FINANCES FOR SMALL-SCALE INDUSTRY
IN INDIA

FINANCES FOR SMALL-SCALE INDUSTRY IN INDIA

by

K. T. RAMAKRISHNA

M.A., M.LITT., PH.D.

Reader in Economics, Osmania University

ASIA PUBLISHING HOUSE

NEW YORK

PRINTED IN INDIA

By Z. T. Bandukwala at Leaders Press Private Limited, Bombay
and Published by P. S. Jayasinghe, Asia Publishing House, 119
West 57th Street, New York

To

MY FATHER and MOTHER

PREFACE

THIS book is based on my thesis, "Finances for Small-Scale Industry in India," which formed the basis of award of the Ph.D. Degree of the University of Madras in 1960.

In this study, the term "small-scale industry" is interpreted to mean all those industries with capital assets up to Rs. 5 lakhs employing 50 workers, using power, and 100 workers working without power. To further delimit the field of investigation, industries coming within the purview of the Small-Scale Industries Board alone are covered. Industries covered by other organizations, such as the Khadi and Village Industries Commission, the All India Handicrafts Board, the Coir Board, the Silk Board and the State Village Industries Boards, have been excluded from the scope of the present study.

Further, enquiry has been confined to governmental and institutional finance. Non-institutional agencies such as moneylenders and indigenous bankers are excluded. The present study is thus limited to financial assistance by the State in the shape of direct credit under the State Aid to Industries Acts, non-financial assistance in the form of external aids and credit from the State Financial Corporations, the State Bank of India under its pilot scheme, the commercial banks, scheduled and non-scheduled, and co-operative banks.

I am indebted to Dr. M. S. Adiseshiah for the suggestion to undertake this study and to Dr. R. Balakrishna for approving the subject for a doctoral thesis. My thanks are due, in a special measure, to Dr. R. Balakrishna for his encouragement which has been a source of strength and inspiration to me in making this study.

I am beholden to the Reserve Bank of India and the State Bank of India, the Small-Scale Industries Board and the National Small Industries Corporation, the Small Industries Service Institutes and the State Financial Corporations for their co-operation and help. I am thankful to the United States Information Library, Madras, for the books they were kind enough to send me on the financial problems of small business in the United States. I am grateful to Prof. S. V. Ayyar, Director, the Indian Institute of Economics, Dr. R. V. Rao, Deputy Director, Department of Commerce & Industries, Government of Andhra Pradesh, Shri Narasiah,

PREFACE

Director, S.I.S.I., Shri S. C. Sharma, Asst. Director, S.I.S.I., Hyderabad, for their kindness in getting material for my work without which it would have suffered in no small degree.

My debt to all those who spared their time to discuss the subject with me is beyond measure.

In conclusion, I must acknowledge my grateful thanks to Shri V. N. Venkatesham for his secretarial assistance.

K. T. RAMAKRISHNA

Osmania University
Hyderabad (A.P.)
April 1961

CONTENTS

CONTENTS

Let knowledge grow from more to more
And more of reverence in us dwell.

—Tennyson

CHAPTER I

THE CAPITAL AND CREDIT NEEDS OF
SMALL-SCALE INDUSTRIES

FINANCE is the life-blood of business in any productive sphere and
its vital need is doubly realized where it is lacking as in small industry. The importance of finance in this field is as fundamental
as elsewhere. Every problem of the small producer concerning
production or materials, quality or marketing is in the ultimate
analysis a financial one.[1] Adequate finance is a pre-requisite to
proper organization of production and the purchase of raw materials,
investment of capital in manufacture and the ultimate profit from
the venture. However, once the enterprise is set on its feet and becomes well established some of the profits earned might be ploughed
back into business.[2] The producer may with growing prosperity
of his trade spare a proportion of the net revenue for a reserve
fund which can stand him in good stead in an emergency. But
apart from such provision against a rainy day, the producer can
convert his own profits into capital for further investment after
meeting his personal requirements. The business, if made lucrative,
can itself create the means for its future sustenance in the way of
capital derived from profits. The producer will be self-reliant up to
a degree in regard to capital. When capital is found, credit will
come. Capital is the basis for borrowing. In small industries it
has to be provided by the entrepreneur himself.[3] On the strength
of his owned capital he may obtain loans. This may well be true

[1] "The problem of small industries together form a vast complex where the
parts regarding material, production, quality, control, finance, marketing etc.
cannot be solved separately. The credit and finance problems have to be tackled
as a part of the whole programme if they are to be solved. For without proper
finance there will be no efficient planning, nor purchase of material, nor production nor marketing nor any fair profit, the latter in its turn forming the foundation of the finance itself." *Report on Small Industries in India*, International
Planning Team, Ford Foundation, Government of India, Ministry of Finance,
1955, Chapter 3, p. 37.

[2] *Ibid.*

[3] *Ibid.* In medium and large-scale industries capital is provided by shareholders.

in the long run. But the immediate problem is to find the initial capital required to set up in business. Perhaps the producers of some standing in their field who have made good already could themselves provide the needed capital as the foundation for their enterprise but those who have to start from scratch, as a good many of them have to, the necessary capital has to be found for them. They cannot be left to shift for themselves as best they could. This is the crucial financial problem of small industry in India today. The most common complaint in different parts of the country is that about the lack of finance. Very often, however, by this is meant the lack of capital as well as credit since no distinction is made between the two although capital must be owned while credit is borrowed in the shape of long-term and short-term loans, the former to finance fixed assets and the latter to defray current expenses on stock, wages and the like. In industrial countries the craftsman or the small industrialist may start business with some saved capital of his own. By and by with skill and energy and business ability he adds to his capital out of his profits. Depending on his aptitude and creditworthiness, he borrows from friends and relatives and may even enjoy trade-credit on materials and goods from suppliers and distributors if he is honest and reliable enough.[4] Thus in the early stages of his career, private credit from individuals plays an important part in financing small industry. The base for such credit is the owned capital combined with immaterial assets possessed by the borrower in the way of his own character and ability. But, for further development of business through investment in new and improved machinery, erection of a small factory or workshop, institutional credit becomes necessary.[5] It is provided in some countries by banks and the like who supply short-term as well as medium and long-term credit. When small industry is run on modern lines, technically and organizationally, banks regard it as creditworthy. The Swedish commercial banks accommodate small producers who seek credit from them. In 1953 the commercial banks in that country gave loans amounting to Rs. 75 crores to small enterprises which formed 35 per cent of the total credit granted to industry and trade. Among the largest commercial banks of Sweden, AB Svenska Handelsbanken gave in 1948, 18 per cent of its credit to small industry. By 1953 the percentage rose to 28.

[4] *Ibid.*, p. 38.   [5] *Ibid.*, p. 38.

This is an indication of the increasing importance of small industry from the banker's point of view in industrially advanced communities. But, this should be viewed in the context of the general economic development of a country. In developed economies enjoying a high standard of living and per capita income with a wide margin of savings available for capital accumulation as deposits in banks, bank credit to small industry might be made available. But in an under-developed and economically backward nation with a low per capita income and insignificant savings due to the subsistence standard of living, banks are hard put to it to finance any but the most important borrowers who may be deemed by them good clients. However, with the future economic growth of the economy under planned industrial and agricultural development, as the standard of living and per capita income rise, small industry may claim a share of institutional credit from banks.[6] But in the present stage of economic development, however, small producers are in a depressed state due to low productivity consequent on the over-crowding of many branches of industry. Despite considerable skill, due to lack of capital and hence proper equipment in the way of efficient tools, their incomes are low out of which little or no saving may be expected. The general poverty of producers accounts for the absence of owned capital. Hard pressed by want, they live from hand to mouth, selling their wares at uneconomic prices from day to day or week to week depending on their needs. They are not free agents working, as they do, for dealers who have to provide them raw materials and, not infrequently, tools. When they buy their own materials, they have to buy retail losing thereby any saving in the form of concessions which they might have otherwise enjoyed if they had bought in bulk. But their purchases being limited by their petty scale of production, they must forgo commercial economies open to bigger customers. Hence, the cost of production might be lower than it is. On the other hand, marketing through middle men, they do not get a fair price for their products. Thus, cost being higher and revenues lower than they might be, they earn a narrow margin of profit which hardly leaves any surplus after their expenditure which might go towards a capital fund to strengthen their business. Owing to lack of capital, credit is not forthcoming. All this is typical of many traditional

[6] *Ibid.*, p. 38.

small industries like the brass industry in Moradabad, the lock industry in Aligarh and the shoe industry in Agra.[7] Yet another reason for the low income of the small producer is the uneconomic units of production operated without enough power, good tools and modern machines.[8] Under the circumstances, banks in India are apt to avoid giving credit to small industry. It is not the practice of Indian commercial banks to give loans on the security of land and buidings, unlike in other countries. Machinery is not accept- able either, as security for loans to small producers. Thus, due to paucity of loanable funds, the existence of uneconomic produc- tive units lacking capital which alone can command credit, and the general loan policy of banking institutions in the country, small industry is not financed by banks[9] except for the State Bank of India which has in recent years started lending to small industry.

Further the modest loans wanted by small producers to finance their little enterprises are too small for commercial banks to be entertained. Doing business on a bigger scale, as they generally are accustomed to, with large scale industries, to deal with smaller clients proves uneconomical and hence small borrowers do not find favour with such banks.[10] In Japan and countries of Europe, industrial banks furnish long-term and medium-term capital to small industry. But in India, commercial banks do not do so. To the banker liquidity is vital and short-term deposits cannot be locked up in long-term loans. Thus, Indian banks are officially expected to refrain from long-term commitments like the British Joint-Stock Banks which are traditionally given to providing only short-term credit to trade and industry. Being based on the British model, Indian Commercial Banks are equally orthodox. Industrial banking on the Japanese and European lines has not developed with any success in India[11]. Not only long and medium-term credit is not forthcoming from Indian commercial banks, but even short-term

---

[7] *Ibid.*, p. 38.   [8] *Ibid.*, p. 39.

[9] The Indian Industrial Commission of 1916-18 called attention to this in its report: *The Indian Industrial Commission Report* 1916-18, Chapter 17, pp. 178-9. P. C. Jain, *Problems in Indian Economic*, 1956, Chapter 17, p. 266.

[10] P. C. Jain, *Problems in Indian Economics*, 1956, p. 266

[11] R. S. Bhatt, Managing Director, Bombay State Financial Corporation, "Finances for Small Industries," *Journal of the Indian Institute of Bankers,* April 1956, p. 17.

credit to small-scale concerns is given by few banks.[12] The minor role of commercial banks in the finance of small industry in India is confirmed by various surveys conducted in the country at different times. The share of small industry in the total advances of scheduled banks as revealed by the 1952 survey of the Reserve Bank of India is given below:[13]

ALL SCHEDULED BANKS-PERCENTAGE OF TOTAL ADVANCES TO VARIOUS INDUSTRIES ACCORDING TO SIZE GROUP OF FIRMS

	Firms with Assets up to (Rs. in lakhs)			
Industry (group)	1	1-5	5-20	20 & above
General Average (all industries)	3.0	7.8	13.6	75.6

It will be seen that small firms got only 10.8 per cent of the total industrial advances given by all the scheduled banks during the year. Of this, firms with assets up to 1 lakh claimed 3.0 per cent while those with assets from 1 to 5 lakhs 7.8 per cent.

Even surveys confined to limited areas point to a similar tendency in commercial banks. A survey of 153 small engineering firms in 1953 by B.I.S. (Calcutta) revealed the following position.[14]

Credit Sources	Percentage to Total Credit
1. Moneylenders	50.7
2. Commercial Banks	18.9
3. Others	30.4

Similarly a survey of 32 engineering firms by the Department of Economics, University of Bombay in 1957 showed the still greater insignificance of commercial bank lending to small producers. The comparative position of various sources of credit is revealed in the following table:[15]

[12] Ibid., p. 18.
[13] C. K. Shah, "Commercial Banks and Finance for Small Industries in India," The Journal of the Indian Institute of Bankers, October 1957, p. 13.
[14] Ibid., p. 13.   [15] Ibid., p. 14.

CREDIT SOURCES—PERCENTAGE DISTRIBUTION

Employment			Credit Sources				
Group	Range	Relatives	Money-lenders	Commercial Banks	Direc-tors	Paya-bles	Others
I.	50.100	6.6	22.8	19.6	2.5	46.2	2.4
II.	20.50	14.2	33.0	6.1	11.1	26.6	9.0
III.	Below 20	29.2	13.2	2.5	3.9	49.1	2.1
AVERAGE		12.5	27.0	11.2	6.9	36.6	5.7

The position in Bombay and Calcutta may be taken as representative of conditions elsewhere as the two cities have sound banking systems and are important centres of small-scale industry.

There are several good reasons why financial institutions like commercial banks are prejudiced against small industries and avoid lending them. The recent experience of the Bombay Financial Corporation reveals various short-comings in these which are to blame for the lack of finance in this sector from institutional sources. Not a few of them fail to qualify for loans. The mortgage offered as security is inadequate. The value of the assets is disproportionate to the amount of the loan and hence cannot be accepted without considerable risk to the lending agency. This is aggravated further by the changing fortunes of the small producers. In times of economic depression, especially, more firms go out of business than come into it. Their instability and precarious existence are hardly calculated to inspire confidence. Apart from these external forces which are often beyond the control of small firms, there are many internal weaknesses which are amenable to correction. Thus, the accounts of some small concerns leave much to be desired. They are neither maintained nor audited according to approved principles. In one-man concerns and partnerships, often, personal accounts and business accounts are mixed up. This is very unbusiness like. Yet another failing brought to light has been lack of a depreciation fund to provide against depreciation of fixed assets, such as building and plant. Banks and others, under these circumstances, cannot possibly give any loans to such borrowers. Their own funds come from private and public savings and they are answerable to their depositors and investors for the use which they make of their borrowed resources. Hence, unless the party concerned has first class mortgage to offer (whose net value is more than the sum desired as loan in order to cover the risk adequately) and is creditworthy and shows promise of investing the capital raised profitably to earn enough revenue for the repayment of the principal and the payment of interest, no responsible credit institution can lend him money. If it does not oblige, it is obviously because the intending borrower lacks proper security or mismanages his business, he is heavily indebted already or not creditworthy.[16]

In the days before the economic transition, India was a land of self-sufficient, tiny village communities. Every village had its band of artisans which supplied the needs of the community. The market did not extend beyond the confines of the village. Demand was consequently limited. What is more important, it was known before hand and hence assured. Little risk or uncertainty was involved in production as it was based on known needs of customers who were in close touch with their suppliers. No barriers of distance and time separated the producer and the consumer. Their relations were close and personal. As such, no problems of marketing as they exist now, troubled the sellers. The modest demand for capital and credit for the production of goods was easily met by the local money-lender. The needed raw materials were provided by consumers and with simple tools and native skill the artisan fashioned useful commodities for the use of his patrons. Often, payment for articles sold was in kind, like rent-free land for the use of the artisans or a proportion of agricultural produce given as the price of the purchase. Under such a simple economic organization, no acute problem of finance could exist for small-scale industry. In towns with their larger populations and bigger markets, the supply of industrial products had of necessity to be more and the need for credit and capital was greater but artisans and craftsmen depended for their credit on guilds which could raise enough finance from their members and if necessary, they borrowed from moneylenders. Thus, both rural and urban industrialists were sufficiently supplied with necessary resources to pursue their productive activities without any hindrance.[17] The economic transition has, however, completely

[16] R. S. Bhatt, Managing Director, Bombay State Financial Corporation, "Finances for Small Industry," *The Journal of the Institute of Bankers*, April 1956, pp. 21-2.

[17] G. M. Laud, *Co-operative Banking in India*, 1956, p. 530.

altered the situation and has brought in its wake a different economic organization (characterized by economic dependence of larger and larger communities on each other, extension of markets, production in anticipation of demand, separation of the buyer and the seller by space and time, fierce competition of the factory industry pushing out the small producer) and the diverse problems concerning him which hinge ultimately on finance for his survival and future prosperity. While organized large-scale industry has solved the problem of finance through corporate business organization, such a source is not open to small-scale industry.

Unproductive debt presents yet another problem as in agriculture—the problem of repayment. When small producers procure short-term credit for current expenses in production like the purchase of raw materials and the like, often they spend it on consumption expenditure instead of investing it as they should.[18] This is obviously due to lack of other means to meet their daily needs of subsistence and occasionally ceremonies, religious and otherwise, which make claims on their meagre income. The credit is thus used to supplement their slender resources and ultimately it becomes a dead-weight debt due to which further credit becomes difficult to obtain. This is a similar situation to what obtains in agriculture where consumption-credit is common enough and is not an insignificant element in the vast rural indebtedness of farmers as a class. The use of co-operative credit given by village societies bears out this fact. If the loans secured were utilised for the legitimate productive purpose for which they are ostensibly raised, they would themselves create the means in the form of value produced by the investment of the loans as capital out of which repayment of borrowed funds becomes possible and indebtedness will not stand in the way of further accommodation by lenders. Thus, added to the lack of reasonable owned capital as the foundation for credit is the existence of prior debts which renders borrowing even more difficult, in an already difficult situation. There is a further similarity between the peasant and the artisan. Like that of the peasant, the income of the artisan is often irregular as the demand for some of his products is seasonal. In a few cases customers take delivery of goods and pay for them on auspicious days. Iron safes, bronze bulls and images thus yield an irregular income to their pro-

[18] Chitra and Viswanath, *Cottage Industries of India*, 1948, p. 126.

ducers.[19] Hence, when they do not earn, they spend the loans got for production on consumption. And consumption-debt accumulates unlike productive debt rendering repayment more and more difficult and defaults on the part of borrowers prejudice chances of further loans.

When loans given are on personal security and not on the security of tangible assets, such as materials or finished products like cotton or cotton cloth, credit is limited to small amounts. But, where larger sums are required to invest in machinery, buildings and so on, as in the case of iron-safe making or hosiery industry, the borrower cannot get the necessary loan and is consequently handicapped'[20] Being poor, very often, he has little security to offer in the shape of material assets even if the creditor is prepared to oblige him with credit on the strength of such security.[21] Household-utensils or brass and silver ornaments are the only security he can produce.[22]

There are several sources of credit open to small industry which are broadly divisible into two kinds, Institutional credit and non-institutional credit. The Contribution of institutional agencies like State Governments and co-operative societies to the finances of small industry is inconsiderable. Small industry depends largely on private agencies for its finance. They are the moneylender, the merchant and the master-craftsman who, between them, supply the bulk of the funds required.[23] Short-term credit comes from moneylenders for the purchase of raw materials and consumption-expenditure. The rate of interest charged is high. However, the borrower usually does not have to surrender his rights over his product to the moneylender as he often has to do when indebted to the merchant or dealer who sells materials to the artisan on credit at a high rate of interest on condition that the finished product is eventually sold through him by his client. This may not be universally true. L. C. Jain has pointed out that the debtor becomes virtually a slave of the moneylender as illustrated by the weaving industry in Northrn India where weavers are indebted to moneylenders who exploit them for their own ends and keep them under

[19] *Ibid.*, p. 126.
[20] Chitra and Viswanath, *Cottage Industries of India*, 1948, p. 126.
[21] P. C. Jain, *Problems in Indian Economics*, 1956, p. 266.
[22] L. C. Jain, *Indigenous Banking in India*, 1929, p. 49.
[23] *All India Rural Credit Survey Report*, 1954, Vol. II, p. 117.

their thumb through threats, intimidation and physical violence.[24] Thus, short-term credit either in the form of cash or raw materials sold on credit is provided by moneylenders and dealers to producers, often to the disadvantage of the latter due to unjust terms on which the bargain is struck between the parties to the transaction. But the subservience of the producer is even greater in his relations with the master-craftsman or *karkhanadar*. In a manner of speaking, the long-term finance is provided by the master-craftsman not as a loan given away to the borrower as a free agent to invest in capital assets on his own but in the form of workshop, capital equipment, material and supplementary finance with which the client engages in production, working under the master-craftsman. As such, he ceases to be an independent producer and becomes virtually a wage-earner losing his freedom in the process.[25] The categories, moneylender, merchant and master-craftsman are not necessarily mutually exclusive and might overlap, so that we may generalise that a debtor to one or the other credit agency loses his freedom in seeking financial assistance from any of them. The measure of control wrongfully gained may be of varying degrees under which the producer as debtor has to function as a tool in the hands of his creditor.

The problem of finance in small-scale industry is a part of the larger problem of providing external aids which are lacking in that sector. Mere finance in the shape of capital and credit is of no avail. It must go along with efficient production and good materials, superior quality and sound marketing. This would imply the need for scientific and technical and administrative assistance besides financial. Many of these difficulties have cropped up in recent years owing to the haphazard growth of small enterprises. During the war and post-war years, small industry flourished. Consumer goods, spare parts and intermediate products of various kinds were in short supply and small producers could profitably provide a good part of those commodities. A sellers' market in the boom conditions of the War enabled them to earn fair profits. With the return of peace and a buyers' market and the revival of competition from large-scale industry, small producers suffered a set-back and encountered a variety of problems relating to organization and efficient equipment, technical guidance and marketing. It is, there-

[24] L. C. Jain, *Indigenous Banking in India*, 1929, p. 50.
[25] *Ibid.*, p. 117.

fore, a complex situation and monetary assistance alone cannot adequately remedy the many ills that small-scale industry suffers from. Lack of finance may be at the root of them. But external aids are necessary to help the small industry use the funds provided to maximum advantage. It is in this sense that finance must be supplemented by other forms of external aid. By himself the small producer is not self-sufficient in regard to technical knowledge, organization or marketing of products. Therefore, along with money these must be forthcoming.[26]

Small industries are generally owned and controlled by individual proprietors or partners or at best, a limited number of shareholders. The owners are often managers as well as financiers of their concerns. As such, the success of the business is conditioned by the aptitude and resources of the entrepreneurs which must inevitably be limited. Many advantages of large-scale production are hence denied to them and they cannot cope with the unequal contest in the powerful rivalry of large-scale units. Unfair competition naturally has a crippling effect on them. Financial strength and protection against overwhelming competition are indicated.[27]

Small-scale industry requires two kinds of capital. (1) Equity or risk capital. (2) Borrowed capital. Borrowed capital consists of: (a) long-term capital for investment in equipment and other capital assets and (b) short-term capital for current needs of industry.

Normally, equity or risk capital is owned by the promoters. It may sometimes be supplemented by funds of friends and relatives in the form of medium-term deposits. The bulk of such capital is invested in fixed assets such as land, buildings and plant. Any surplus left over is used as working capital. A study of a representative group of small industries in the State of Bombay showed that many of them were under-capitalized. And even if some start with adequate capital to begin with, with the growth of the industry, they run short of it. Thus, lack of equity capital presents one problem of finance in regard to small-scale industry in the country. The average investor in the money market is not interested in small enterprises and he is of little help in getting

[26] R. S. Bhatt, Managing Director, Bombay State Financial Corporation, "Finances for Small Industries," *The Journal of the Institute of Bankers*, April 1956, pp. 15, 23.

[27] *Ibid.*, pp. 15, 16.

such capital from the market. Even if investors might be persuaded to come to the aid of small producers, on their part small entrepreneurs themselves do not care to entertain any equity capital from outside as it would inevitably necessitate sharing their management and control which they do not like. Hence, there is the need for an agency to provide risk capital to small producers.

Besides risk capital, long-term capital is needed for purposes of expansion of the units, renovation of plant and modernization of machinery and short-term credit for working capital or current finance to buy raw materials and stores, pay wages, hold stocks of finished goods, etc. Neither of these is given by commercial banks in India, unlike banks abroad. Small-scale industry has to fall back upon the aid of the state under the State Aid to Industries Acts and State Financial Corporations for their long-term and medium-term credit requirements and moneylenders and indigenous bankers for short-term loans at high rates of interest.[28] Sometimes, small industries enjoy the advantage of trade-credit when they buy raw materials and stores. But the effect of this is neutralized as they have to sell their goods on credit to their customers like large-scale producers. In the process of waiting for payments, they run short of money for current expenditure. The need for working capital becomes so acute that not a few firms are hard put to it to carry on. In recent years, this aspect of the financial problem of small-scale industry has become especially severe.[29]

[28] *Ibid.*, pp. 16-18.   [29] *Ibid.*, pp. 18, 19.

CHAPTER II

THE STATE AND SMALL-SCALE INDUSTRIES

THE assistance of the State, at various levels, Central and Provincial, to small-scale industries is of two kinds: financial and non-financial. Financial aid is in the form of credit to small-scale industries. Non-financial aid, in the form of technical assistance and marketing, supply of raw materials and machinery, water and power, transport and factory buildings, is of basic importance, as technical efficiency and marketability of goods, earning capacity and ability to repay loans determine the creditworthiness of small-scale industrialists and enable them to borrow from other sources the needed finance for investment. As such, non-financial aid by the state, until such time as the small-scale producer becomes self-reliant for the above facilities and services, is as important as financial aid because it creates credit from other quarters. Non-financial aid, due to its fundamental importance for solving the financial problems of small-scale industries in India and its contribution to the solution of those problems has to be considered in a study of the question of finances for small-scale industry in India.

Financial Aid

Loans are given to small-scale industries by the various State Governments under their respective State Aid to Industries Acts/ Rules. In some States, owing to different sets of rules governing the grant of credit, there is no uniformity: in the state of Andhra Pradesh, the grant of loans to small-scale industries is governed by the Madras State Aid to Industries Act of 1922 and the Hyderabad State Aid (Cottage and Small-Scale) Industries Act of 1956, covering the Andhra and the Telangana regions respectively. Owing to the dual legislation governing the offer of credit by the State Government, the terms vary from one region to the other. Borrowers in Telangana have an advantage over those in Andhra due to the more liberal terms under the Hyderabad Act. In one state such a big difference in terms seems undesirable. One set of rules for the whole of the Andhra Pradesh State seems desirable, for greater uniformity, in the assistance of the government to small-scale industries. Fresh legislation to replace the existing acts is indicated. Under the new act, the terms of loans should be as liberal as they are under the Hyderabad Act, if not more. It is interesting to note that Andhra Pradesh is like Madhya Pradesh, in this respect, where different acts and rules apply to different parts of the state for the grant of loans to small-scale industries. However, in Madhya Pradesh, a new act has been passed to cover the whole state, in order to make the laws relating to state assistance to small-scale industries uniform everywhere.[1]

A study of the procedure for granting loans reveals the elaborate nature of it and the long time taken to give the loan eventually to the applicant. At a conservative estimate, based on an examination of the procedure involved and the time taken at different stages of it, it appears that applicants have to wait for months before they get the loan after sanction. For loans up to Rs. 1,000 the time taken for sanction and disbursement is at least $3\frac{1}{2}$ months. More time is taken in the case of bigger loans. For loans over Rs. 1,000 and up to Rs. 5,000 the time taken for disbursement is at least about 7 months. The time taken to authorize the drawal of the sanctioned amount is about 2 months. Thus, altogether it takes about 9 months to get loans above Rs. 1,000 and up to Rs. 5,000. Hence, for smaller loans, no less than a quarter of an year and for bigger loans, three-quarters of an year are taken for final disbursement to the applicants.[2] The delay in disbursing credit which is common to all the states may be attributed to the State Government authorities as well as the small-scale industrialists. On the side of the State Governments concerned, the delay is avoidable to some extent if cases are disposed of more quickly. Delay due to red-tape could be cut down. Where departments of government concerned with credit to small-scale industries are under-staffed, their staff need to be strengthened. But if the delay is due to scrutiny of loan applications, mortgage-deeds and other important documents, it is inevitable, and can hardly be helped by the government. Even this might be minimized if a separate department of small-scale

---

[1] *Background Papers* 8, Seminar on Financing of Small-Scale Industries in India, Reserve Bank of India, July 1959.
[2] *Ibid.*

industries were opened in each state, which can cover small-scale industries, in the place of the general department of industries and commerce which is, at present, incharge of all industries including small-scale ones. It must, however, be said that a good deal of time is taken in gathering information on the applicant and his business before a loan can be sanctioned. If a census of small-scale industries in each state were taken, and every aspect of each unit is covered by it and brought up-to-date, sanction and disbursement of loans can be speeded up to no small extent. A further measure may be the routing of all state loans through State Financial Corporations or other agencies, like the State Bank of India. The most effective solution to the problems posed by direct credit by the state to small-scale industries seems to be a replacement of credit in cash by non-financial assistance of everykind, from the provision of work-space to the sale of the product. Many of the difficulties inherent in the situation under a system of direct credit by the government, like delay and defaults, overdues and bad debts, could be overcome, which are at present at the root of the conservative policies adopted by the government, as a moneylender to industry. However, until enough industrial estates can be set up to cover all the small-scale units; until the National Small Industries Corporation can extend its operation to meet the demands of every small producer for machinery on hire purchase, cheap raw materials and marketing facilities; and until the net-work of Small Industries Service Institutes is sufficient to promote the technical efficiency and management of the small concern in every nook and corner of the land, credit is indispensable to tide over the transition through which small-scale industries have got to pass before they become fully mature, stable and self-reliant. Therefore, it might be said that direct credit by the State to small-scale industries and non-financial assistance supplement each other.

Non-financial Aid

While financial aid through loans and advances is a direct form of assisting small-scale industries with resources to conduct their productive operations, non-financial aid is an indirect way of doing so, by providing producers goods in the shape of raw materials and machinery, motive power and buildings at lower cost and rendering marketing, managerial and technical services, all of which are vital for success. Indeed, non-financial factors are a pre-requisite not only for developing creditworthiness in small-scale industrialists without which they cannot command credit in the money-market but also for enabling them to utilize the loans, given by the State under the State Aid to Industries Acts & Rules in various parts of the country, to maximum advantage. In the absence of adequate materials and machinery, technical competence and efficient marketing, factory building and cheep power, the borrowers who may get credit from the government are apt to misuse the funds, often due to sheer inability to put them to proper use. Instances of misuse of funds have come to light. Non-financial aid is being given by the government, in India, through various agencies: technical guidance and management training are given through the Small Industries Service Institutes; marketing facilities, materials and machinery, through the National Small Industries Corporation and industrial facilities like water and power, transport and communication, workspace and technical assistance, through industrial estates.

Government Purchase

Under its scheme of securing orders for small-scale industries from the government for their products the National Small Industries Corporation acts as an intermediary between the producers and the State as consumer. The trend of contracts secured by small units with the assistance of the Corporation from the government, as revealed by statistical evidence, has been encouraging.[3] In view of the success of the Corporation in its efforts to promote government patronage, other government organizations are being approached by it for contracts to small-scale industries. One notable example is the Railway Board which has agreed to purchase stores for the railways from small producers. The State Governments have also been approached to purchase their stores from small-scale industries and some of the State Governments have since been doing so. In order to cover as many small-scale industries as possible, the Small Industries Service Institutes screen them to select units which are eligible for participation in the Government

[3] See Appendix A.

Purchase Scheme and enlist new members continuously. As a result of these efforts the number of small-scale units coming under the Scheme has increased.[4] Besides the small-scale units enlisted with the Small Industries Service Institutes, some unregistered small-scale units were certified to be competent by the National Small Industries Corporation to supply the government and were given contracts. There has been a progressive increase in the number of such units. Under the Scheme certain items of stores are exclusively reserved for purchase from small-scale units by the government. Further, in order to encourage small-scale industries the government gave a price preference up to 15 per cent over the quotations of large-scale producers to small units. To help them execute the contracts from the government the National Small Industries Corporation has arranged for technical and financial assistance to small-scale units. In producing goods according to specifications, small-scale industries are advised and aided by the Small Industries Service Institutes in various parts of the country.[5] The National Small Industries Corporation arranged with the State Bank of India, under its Pilot Scheme, for loans to small-scale units, to buy raw materials for the production of goods ordered by the government. Under this scheme, the State Bank of India, since 1 January 1959, has agreed to open cash-credit accounts for small-scale units recommended by the Corporation and to give credit against the security of the raw materials. Due to the extension of the Pilot Scheme of the State Bank to all its branches, it is expected that more cash-credit loans for the execution of government orders by small-scale industries will be given by the Bank to applicants in need of such help. The limited progress under the credit-facility scheme may partly be due to the infancy of the scheme and the unawareness of small-scale producers of the liberal terms offered under it. As the scheme becomes known more widely, it may be expected to become more popular.

Small-Scale Units As Ancillaries

The National Small Industries Corporation finds customers for small producers, further, among large-scale industries which can

[4] See Appendix B.
[5] *Bulletin of Small Industries*, No. 14, April 1959.

regularly buy their components and parts from them. Such an arrangement has commerical significance for small-scale industries. It ensures regular custom and provides a market for the products of small-scale industries as ancillaries. The Corporation has been trying to extend the market for small-scale industries by developing ancillary industries by promoting the growth of existing ones and establishing new ones both in the public and private sectors of the economy.[6] To this end steps have been taken to reach agreement with large-scale industries for placing orders with small-scale ancillary units for their requirements.[7] The Corporation also provides every facility to the ancillaries to execute such contracts to the satisfaction of their patrons. As a result of the efforts made by the Corporation and Small Industries Service Institutes, it has been arranged to set up ancillary units to supply components and parts to large-scale industries.[8] Some industries have agreed to the proposal of small-scale ancillaries to feed them and schemes for setting them up are under way. While agreement has been reached in the above cases, the Corporation is negotiating with other large-scale industries to develop more small-scale ancillary industries.[9] Although some progress has been made in this regard, it could be better. The tardy rate of progress may be attributed to the backwardness of small-scale industries and lack of confidence in them on the part of large-scale industries. In the course of time, as small-scale industries improve and turn out quality products, they may win over customers who resist their offer of goods now. The significance of the scheme to develop small-scale ancillaries in the country lies in the fact that some of the small-scale industries will have an assured market for their products.

Marketing

Although the state is the most important single largest buyer in the country, it cannot patronize so many producers in the small-scale

---

[6] *Third Annual Report*, 1957-58, National Small Industries Corporation, p. 8.

[7] *Agenda Papers* IV (*d*), Seminar of Financing of Small-Scale Industries in India, Reserve Bank of India, July 1959.

[8] *Ibid.*

[9] *Agenda and Notes*, Thirteenth Meeting of Small-Scale Industries Board, May 1959.

sector. They must turn to the general public to patronize them. Hence, apart from the contracts obtained from the government, Central and State, for the small-scale industries, the Corporation finds markets for them at home and abroad. There is a large potential market in rural and urban areas within the country and markets overseas. In India itself there are 300 million potential buyers in the villages and 60 million in towns to absorb the output of small-scale industries.[10] This is specially so under the planned development of the country which will generate income and purchasing power in the future. However, owing to shortcomings like lack of standardization, a trade-name and contact with markets[11] small-scale producers are unable to reach such customers. Often small-scale units are obliged to dispose of their wares soon after production. For example, small-scale leather units have to sell their finished goods at nightfall to pay for materials next morning as they lack working capital and cannot hold their articles but have to sell them to middlemen. Sometimes, products of small-scale industries, such as cutlery, are produced at a sufficiently low cost to sell in the world market at competitive prices and yet they lack markets.[12] This is because they do not go beyond local markets. Lack of communications is partly responsible for it and ignorance of possible consumers farther afield.[13]

In the long run, co-operative marketing will have to solve the marketing prolems of small-scale industries. Immediately, however, they need help from the State which is being given by the National Small Industries Corporation.

The scheme of mobile sales van operations was tried as an experiment by the Corporation and it proved unsuccessful due to practical difficulties encountered in working it. The mobile vans were intended partly for promoting sales of small-scale industries' products and partly to give publicity to those products and collect marketing data. At the Small Scale Industries Board meeting held at Srinagar, the latter functions of the vans were stressed and considered primary while the promotion of sales as only secondary to them. However, since the results of the van operation did not justify the cost of the

---

[10] *Report on Small Industries in India*, Ford Foundation Team, 1955.
[11] *Third Annual Report*, 1957-58, National Small Industries Corporation.
[12] Small Industries Corporation, *A Brief Survey*, 1955-56.
[13] *Report on Small Industries in India*, Ford Foundation Team, 1955.

scheme, it was discontinued from April 1959. If research and publicity are considered more important than sales promotion, it might be worthwhile to resume the scheme of mobile van operations even if it has proved financially a failure. The sales side might be discontinued but the vans might still operate for other purposes which are sure to bear fruit in the long run. Moreover, in the long run, co-operative marketing societies could be developed to market the goods for the small-scale industrialists. Research and publicity may, however, be carried on by means of mobile vans permanently.

In the small-scale sector, there is no standardization. Articles do not have a familiar brand-name to denote the make and quality of the product for the benefit of the consumer who may be able to buy it confidently on the basis of it. Producers have no proper organization for marketing their wares in a wider market where their products may sell. To set right the position the National small Industries Corporation has opened a chain of wholesale depots at various centres where small-scale industries are localized The sales have been steadily rising at all the depots generally and the progress made is encouraging.

Export Promotion

The mobile van operations and wholesale depots covered only the domestic market but not the overseas markets in foreign countries. To develop markets abroad for the small-scale industries the National Small Industries Corporation promotes the export of their products. Sale of such goods overseas depends on their quality and owing to the poor quality of Indian products, they do not sell although their prices may be competitive.[14] To improve their quality and their marketability abroad, the Corporation has selected a few products of small-scale industries for export promotion. Various steps have been taken to give them wide publicity in foreign countries. The products of a variety of small-scale industries have been sent to inter-national exhibitions and trade fairs for display. To advertise the goods abroad, samples are sent to foreign countries. As a result of these measures, some small-scale industries have received orders for goods from abroad through

[14] *Background Papers* 10, Seminar on Financing of Small-Scale Industries in India, Reserve Bank of India, July 1959.

the National Small Industries Corporation. Of the different items selected for export promotion, leather goods as indicated by the total value of sales have won markets abroad. Execution of large orders from the U.S.S.R. and Poland indicates that small-scale leather industries are capable of meeting the demand overseas and satisfying the high standards of quality required there. The success of these industries in foreign markets has been a source of encouragement to them. Similarly, if other small-scale industries achieve some success, they may improve their exports. Trade enquiries and requests for samples and quotations from abroad indicate the growing interest of foreign importers in Indian goods from the small-scale sector and there is room for optimism in regard to their success eventually. In executing orders for leather goods from abroad, to reach the standard desired, technical assistance had to be given to small-scale units which improved their methods of production generally.[15] A similar result may well follow in the case of other items of goods intended for export if they are given technical assistance. The experiment made by the National Small Industries Corporation has proved promising. If the success of the leather industry and the lessons learnt from it are properly followed up, success may be expected in other industries as well. The basic condition for success will be the quality of the goods. If that is mainted, they may well be able to compete in world markets. It is very essential that the quality of the commodities be properly checked before export. Once our small-scale industries establish their reputation for quality, their markets will grow in due course. The importance of quality can hardly be overemphasized. As in the case of the leather industry which responded to technical assistance, other industries may also respond and improve the quality of their products. Among other measures to improve quality, technical aid is indicated.

Hire-purchase of Machinery

On their technical side, small-scale industries are backward. One reason for it is lack of proper machinery. But due to the expense involved in buying it, often, small-scale industries use obsolete machinery. One form of non-financial aid to correct the situation

[15] *Ibid.*

is to provide machinery on a hire purchase basis to enable small-scale producers to buy them and pay for them in convenient instalments spread over a length of time. This has been attempted by the National Small Industries Corporation in its scheme to supply machinery on hire-purchase to small-scale industries in accordance with the recommendations of the Ford Foundation Team. The hire-purchase scheme has been in operation since March 1956. The terms and conditions of hire-purchase were framed with a view to enable a small-scale industrialist of slender means to get machinery on easy terms of payment.

To meet the requirements of small-scale industries, the Corporation needs annually foreign exchange of Rs. 1.3 crores to supply adequate machine-tools to them.[16] Due to lack of sufficient foreign exchange, there is a gap between the orders for machinery from small-scale industrialists and the applications accepted on the one hand and the delivery of machines on the other.[17] To some extent the Corporation has eased the situation by booking orders with domestic manufacturers where possible if such machines were made at home and available.[18] But if they have got to be imported, the Corporation should be given more foreign exchange by the government for the purpose. Unless the machinery is made available to small-scale industries, their technical development will be retarded. In view of the importance of small-scale industries for the general economic development of the economy, foreign exchange should not be a bottle-neck impeding their progress. The alternative to import of machinery would be production at home to make the country self-sufficient in machine-tools needed by small-scale industries. This might be done by developing more proto-type production centres for the manufacture of machines, like the ones at Rajkot and Okhla. Originally, under the hire-purchase scheme of the Corporation, ungraded machines were not supplied. But due to the stringency of foreign exchange and the consequent difficulty of importing foreign machines freely, the Small Scale Industries Board recommended that the National

---

[16] *Background Papers* 10, Seminar on Financing of Small-Scale Industries in India, Reserve Bank of India, July 1959.

[17] *Minutes*, 11th Meeting of the Small-Scale Industries Board, May 1958, p. 13, Ministry of Commerce and Industry, Government of India.

[18] *Third Annual Report*, 1957-58, National Small Industries Corporation, p. 7.

Small Industries Corporation might supply ungraded machines to small-scale industries provided they were of a satisfactory quality and certified as such by a Small Industries Service Institute and specially required by an applicant.

Both in the number of machines delivered and their value, there was progressive increase as indicated by figures for various trends over several years. The growing impact of the scheme is reflected in the progressively rising trend, from year to year, of the orders placed for machines and applications accepted.[19] However, the gap between the percentages for machines accepted for supply by the National Small Industries Corporation and orders placed with manufacturers indicates delay due to various reasons: old applications pending execution by the Corporation, time taken in negotiating with suppliers at home or abroad for the exact machine desired, delay due to correspondence with applicants when close substitutes are available and suggested by the Corporation, delay in payment of earnest money by the applicant and time taken in getting the import licences where foreign machines are involved.[20]

Over the years 1956-59 there was a decline in the number of applications for machinery received by the Corporation caused by a variety of factors:[21] (1) In the course of time, as the novelty of the scheme disappeared, it might have attracted fewer and fewer applicants. In the beginning, some applications must have come just from curious applicants not genuinely interested in getting machinery on hire-purchase but inquisitive to know all about it. But this reason could have been a superficial one and not have carried much weight. Indeed, if the scheme had grown in popularity, the response of small-scale producers to it should have increased and the applications with it.

(2) There were other handicaps which might have prevented small-scale industrialists from taking advantage of the scheme, such as shortage of raw materials, particularly imported ones, shortage of working capital and ignorance of the scheme in smaller industrial towns.

(3) The disappointment of some might have dampened the enthu-

[19] See Appendix C.
[20] Note on the Hire-Purchase System, *Fourth Annual Report*, 1958-59, Nationa Small Industries Corporation.
[21] *Ibid.*

siasm of intending applicants to some extent and stopped them from trying.

(4) The basic cause might have been the delay in deliveries and the small proportion of the number of machines delivered to the total number of machines applied for. Whatever may be the difficulties of the Corporation in accepting applications, placing orders and arranging for the supply of machinery by manufacturers, the applicants judge the success of the scheme by actual delivery of goods. Due to ignorance of the genuine difficulties of the Corporation, they cannot appreciate delay or take an understanding view of the position. They are apt to imagine that they will be disappointed like their colleagues and hence may as well not try at all. This psychology probably explains the waning popularity of the scheme if the number of applicants and the value covered by them is any indication.

If these causes for the lessening response of the public to the scheme were removed, it will improve. In a vast country like India, by extending the scheme to more and more new centres of small-scale industries, the novelty of the scheme can be kept alive. Many people still do not know about it and if they were informed about it, they should take interest in it. Bottle-necks in regard to raw materials, working capital and the like must be removed if small-scale industries are to demand more machinery under the hire-purchase scheme and take advantage of it. To remove the prejudice from the minds of the public, they must be apprised of the difficulties of the Corporation in obtaining machinery due to various reasons. This would alleviate the scepticism of clients and inspire greater confidence in the benefits of the scheme. Above all, more machines should be supplied and without delay. This would change the attitude of the public to the scheme.

For making the scheme more popular, it may be suggested that: (1) greater publicity be given wherever small-scale industries are located. In this connection, it will be worthwhile to use mobile vans to tour the areas and make known to the public the existence of the scheme. (2) The touring personnel may discuss with interested parties the genuine difficulties and problems encountered in obtaining machinery and win over the sceptics. (3) Increased efforts should be made to get over shortages of materials and working capital. If more materials and working capital become available, the need for machinery will be more keenly felt and demand for it will inevitably increase. Provision of materials and capital is of basic importance and their supply should be promoted through greater efforts by the State by means of its agencies and others. Thus more working capital should be given by financial agencies on the strength of the Corporation's hire-purchase scheme. The Corporation itself should redouble its efforts to increase the supply of raw materials which are in short supply. (4) To restore confidence in the scheme, it may be better to accept fewer applications in order to reduce the gap between accepted applications and the number of deliveries. (5) In the short run, more ungraded machines may be supplied and to this end, difficulties faced by the Corporation such as testing facilities and others must be overcome. Greater foreign allocation should be sought from the government to increase imported machinery required in the small-scale sector. (6) To a large extent the gap between machines promised and ordered could be removed by making them at home. More proto-type production centres are indicated to make machines on foreign models. Until the proto-type production-cum-training centres at Okhla and Rajkot go into operation in 1960-61 and produce tools, the foreign exchange position will obstruct adequate imports of machinery by the Corporation for supply to small-scale industries.

The effect of the hire-purchase scheme may be seen in the developments in the small-scale sector. Various units in light engineering, chemical and wood-working industries have expanded their output, diversified their products and improved their quality. New units have been opened due to the availability of machinery under the scheme. The number of units, volume of employment and volume of output recorded an increase in all the four regions, Northern, Southern, Western and Eastern, after the installation of machinery supplied on hire-purchase by the Corporation.[22]

The results of the evaluation of the hire-purchase scheme carried out by the Corporation in the different regions have brought to light the significant fact that shortage of materials or power and the existence of labour trouble render machinery ineffective. Due to them, production cannot commence even though a unit may be well-equipped. The causes for the tardy progress of the hire-purchase scheme since its inception as revealed by statistical data

[22] See Appendix D.

can be traced to lack of materials and power and labour unrest besides the failings of the scheme itself discussed above.

Industrial Estates

Besides finance and machinery, small-scale industries need facilities like means of transport and communications, motive power and lighting, water and factory space, gas and steam, compressed air and watch and ward. These are normally available in bigger towns and cities in India. To avail himself of them, the small-scale producer migrates to such places, further crowding congested industrial districts. To disperse small-scale industries far and wide and keep them away from existing centres of production and closer to sources of raw materials and markets, such facilities should be provided to them. By so doing, small-scale units will be more evenly distributed over the country. Their proximity to materials and markets will obviate some transport costs and their dispersal will provide employment to more people.[23] With this in mind, industrial estates are being established in India by the State on the lines of Trade Estates in Great Britain which were highly effective in reviving depressed industries during the inter-war years.

The various handicaps of the small-scale industrialist which have been discussed are removed by the industrial estates. They create what might correspond to external and internal economies of large-scale production in the sphere of small-scale production as small-scale industries lack such economies due to their size. Thus, in India small-scale industrialists lack capital to buy sites and erect factories. Even if capital is found, they encounter practical difficulties in acquiring a proper site, getting the sanction of municipal and other authorities for their plans, constructing buildings according to health-laws and factory-rules and getting water and power. Such obstacles discourage ambitious and enterprising individuals from opening industries of their own or expanding existing ones. An industrial estate provides buildings for factories, water and power, railway sidings and wharfs, post offices and telephone exchanges, insurance offices and employment exchanges, banks and hospitals, canteens and clubs and reading rooms and shops. In addition, they render services like heat-treatment and metal-

[23] Small Industries Corporation, *A Brief Survey*, 1955-56.

testing, electro-plating and enamelling and case-hardening and tool manufacture. A cluster of small units withing the estates can co-operate in buying materials and selling finished products to their mutual benefit. Further, they may have the benefit of machinery on hire-purchase, a marketing organization through wholesale depots and contracts from the government under the programme of the National Small Industries Corporation, technical assistance and advice from the Small Industries Service Institutes and credit from State Governments. In short, all the facilities for production and amenities of social life are made available for their health and efficiency.

For extensive industrial development in India under economic planning, promotion of decentralized small-scale industries has become necessary to cover as much area as possible and give employment and produce goods to meet the needs of the country in the short run. Industrial estates help in working out such a plan.

For the industrial development of rural areas, rural community workshops are being planned by the government. They correspond to industrial estates but operate on a smaller scale, providing similar facilities to small-scale industries in rural areas.

The actual working of the industrial estates has brought to light some difficulties suffered by small-scale units located in them. Surveys have revealed that production of a number of units was at a low level for want of raw materials, especially iron and hard coke, which are in short supply throughout the country.[24] Some units have suspended their operations for the same reason. Secondly, technical assistance which is one of the principal services expected is lacking in the estates which must be a deterrent to progress. Thirdly, the products of the units are of a poor quality as necessary arrangements for the inspection of products are absent. Fourthly, tenants in the estates complain of high rents for their accommodation. Fifthly, in some estates individual plots and sheds are too large for a small-scale unit which is uneconomical. To benefit the maximum number of small-scale producers, the size of the plots and sheds should be consistent with their requirements of space.

As on 31 December, 1958, in the 16 industrial estates completed, there were 581 sheds. It is significant that of them only 313 or

[24] *Background Papers* 2, Seminar on Financing of Small-Scale Industries in India, Reserve Bank of India, July 1959.

approximately 54 per cent were occupied.[25] The record in most of the States as revealed by statistics was poor. The vacant sheds amounting to 46 per cent of the total number of sheds constructed in the country might have been due to unawareness or inability on the part of small-scale industrialists to take advantage of the estates. As in the case of the Rajkot estate, high rents or lack of raw materials and technical assistance might have been responsible for it. These shortcomings probably disappointed eager producers and their dissatisfaction prevented others from coming forward. If lack of housing is a serious handicap, this must be a factor which accounts for unoccupied sheds.[26] However, it would seem that industrial estates, in spite of the numerous facilities promised by them, are unable to help small-scale industries to fill up all the sheds. For lack of precise information, it has not been possible to determine the exact causes of the phenomenon. If it is only due to the fact that industrial estates are still new and in a conservative community it takes time for people to take kindly to them, there is no cause for concern. If, however, other factors such as those mentioned above are keeping the public from coming forward,until they are removed, industrial estates will be slow in achieving their objective of the planned development of small-scale industries in India. On the other hand, in Okhla 700 industrialists applied for allotment but only 74 were accommodated.[27] This indicates the ineligibility of the rest.

The causes of slow progress in industrial estates must be removed through the following measures: more raw materials, especially iron and coke, must be made available to the units in the estates. More technical assistance from the Small Industries Service Institutes and the Industrial Extension Service is indicated. This deficiency will be made up when all the 64 Industrial Extension Service Centres are opened.[28] At present there are only 16 Extension Centres[29] and hence there is lack of adequate technical assistance. Improvement of quality in the products of the units in the estates should be brought about by quality-control. To ensure good quality

[25] *Ibid.*
[26] *Minutes*, 13th Meeting of the Small Scale Industries Board, May 1959.
[27] Small Industries Corporation, *A Brief Survey*, 1955-56.
[28] Industrial Extenstion Service, Small-Scale Industries.
[29] *Ibid.*

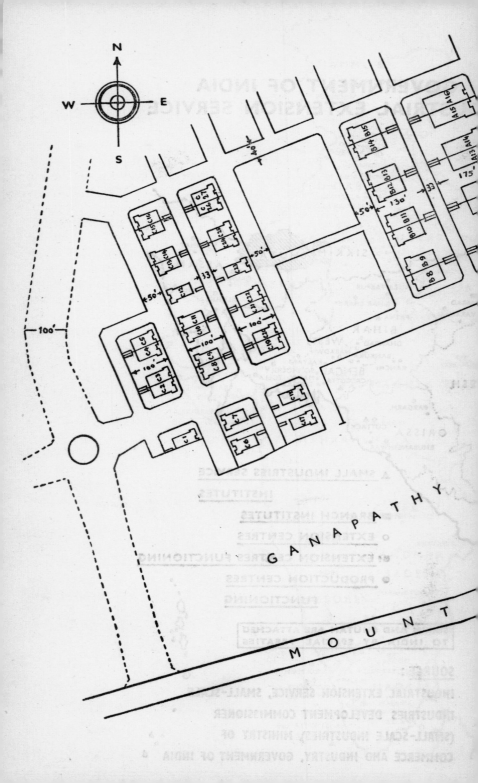

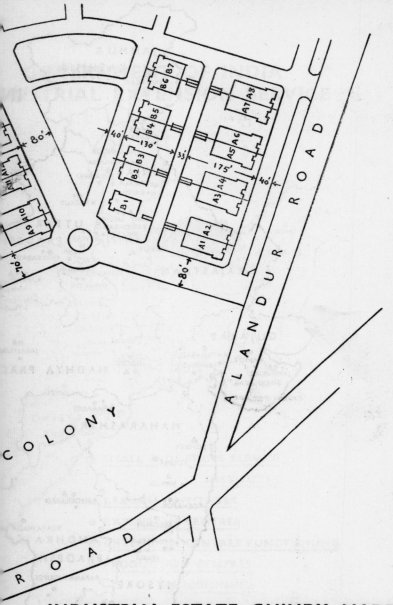

INDUSTRIAL ESTATE, GUINDY, MADRAS.

SITE PLAN

SOURCE: "SMALL INDUSTRY" SOUVENIR SPECIAL
ISSUE VOLUME II, No. 1, 7th JANUARY 1958
THE SMALL SCALE INDUSTRIES ASSOCIATION, MADRAS.

and standard products, all the goods made in the estates may be distributed through the net-work of wholesaling offices which should accept only goods of quality bearing a trade mark like "Jan Sevak." The Small Industries Service Institutes and Industrial Extension Service Centres could also help through their quality marking and testing sections. It was pointed out that workshops in the estates were too large for tenants. This must be responsible for prohibitive rents. If the units are reduced in size, rents will come down. The experience at Okhla indicates a high percentage of small-scale producers who were ineligible for admission into the estate. A liberal policy for admission might perhaps help in giving industrial estates a start. Once they get going, incompetent units may be eliminated in due course as new tenants will be found with the greater popularity of the estates. Living quarters for workers and tenants will also facilitate occupation of estates. Labour colonies as in the Guindy Estate at Madras will help the estate fill up to capacity. The correction of these defects must make the estates more attractive to intending tenants and buyers.

By and by, as the various shortcomings and handicaps which are inevitable in every pioneering effort are got over, industrial estates will work better. Indeed, the present target of over 100 estates is far from enough. Soon, thousands of estates will be needed as industrialization gets under way. But in the long run, the State alone will not be able to construct all the estates needed. Private enterprise and co-operative societies will have to undertake their construction as in the United Kingdom where the State, private enterprise and co-operative societies have all built trade estates with notable success.[30]

Despite their failings, industrial estates have helped in increasing employment and production.

Small-scale industries lack among other things technical knowledge. They do not generally have the benefit of the services of hired technicians or business consultants to guide and advise them on technical and managerial questions connected with their business.[31] The bulk of them carry on production with traditional techniques which are out of place in industry today. Owing to the obsolete

[30] *Small Industries Information Series No. 2*, Industrial Estates.
[31] *Background Papers* 7, Seminar on Financing of Small-Scale Industries in India, Reserve Bank of India, July 1959.

methods in use, the products of small-scale industries tend to be expensive to make and poor in quality.[32] These attributes put them at a disadvantage in competition with the products of large-scale industries which enjoy the advantage of up-to-date and superior techniques that cut down the costs of production of the commodity and at the same time improve its quality. To remove the handicaps of the small-scale units, the State provides free technical service which is normally beyond the means of such units. This is done under the Industrial Extension Service of the Government of India through the Small Industries Service Institutes and the Industrial Extension Service Centres.

More and more industries in the small-scale sector are using the facilities offered by the Industrial Extension Service as indicated by statistical data for a series of years.[33]

As a result of the technical assistance given by technical officers and foreign consultants, there has been an improvement in techniques of production and the quality, and finish of goods, and goods are being produced at a lower cost than before.

---

[32] Industrial Extension Service, Small-Scale Industries.
[33] See Appendix E.

CHAPTER III

THE STATE FINANCIAL CORPORATIONS AND SMALL-SCALE INDUSTRIES

THE bulk of the credit given by the State Financial Corporations goes to large-scale and medium-scale industries and only about a third is obtained by small-scale industries. There are several reasons why small-scale industries get such a minor share in the total credit supplied by the Corporations to industry. From an analysis of the working of some of the Corporations it appears that by and large small-scale industries are not creditworthy and they fail to fulfil the requisite conditions to qualify for loans.[1] It has been the experience of the Kerala Financial Corporation that small-scale industries are inherently weak from the point of their financial structure and resources, and therefore, cannot be trusted with long-term credit. This is confirmed by the fact that the majority of the defaulters were small-scale industries. Of the defaulters, all except one were small-scale units. Financial difficulties of the proprietors of small-scale concerns, change of management and ownership, reverses in trade were often responsible for defaults.[2] Even though the Kerala Financial Corporation has a creditable record in regard to assistance to small-scale industries, of late there has been a decline in the loans to small-scale industries because of want of required security with borrowers to pledge and their inability to comply with the terms of the loan.[3]

Similarly, the Punjab Financial Corporation has met with various difficulties, legal, financial and practical, in offering credit to small-scale industries. They lack fixed assets of sufficient value to offer as security, clear title to the assets which may serve as pledge for credit, and the ability to bear legal and other charges like stamp duty and registration fees. These numerous handicaps of small-scale industries limit the operations of the

[1] *Background Papers* 3, Seminar on Financing of Small-Scale Industries in India, Reserve Bank of India, July 1959.

[2] *Sixth Annual Report*, 1959, Kerala Financial Corporation.

[3] Chairman's Speech, Sixth Annual General Meeting, Kerala Financial Corporation, 1959.

31

Corporation.[4] On the other hand, the Corporation was able to help medium-scale industries as they were eligible for credit.[5] It might be inferred, therefore, that most of the applications for credit which had to be rejected must have been those of small-scale industries and the reasons for rejection were many, such as the absence of sufficient security and scope for expansion of the industries, want of capacity to earn profits and repay the principal and interest, unsound financial position, adverse credit reports and inefficient management.[6]

For giving long-term credit, the Corporation encounters still other difficulties. The applicants who seek loans possess no proper accounts of their business. The ledgers are often in the nature of scrolls which do not disclose the exact financial position of the intending borrower. There are numerous errors and facts are concealed. There are no vouchers or accounts in respect of land, buildings and machinery offered as security. The applicants are suspicious and do not take the Corporation fully into their confidence. Such an unhelpful and non-co-operative attitude on the part of borrowers is not favourable in considering loan applications. Sometimes concerns which approach the Corporation have no clear status or constitution. Joint-families which break up do not possess proper partition deeds. Partnerships are formed and dissolved without partnership and dissolution deeds and documents for the settlement of accounts between partners. Such an anomalous position of applicants is yet another deterrent factor.[7]

Among the general difficulties experienced by the State Financial Corporations was the lack of statistical data on demand, installed capacity and production of industries, which (data) are vital to assess the prospects of borrowing concerns. Further, small-scale industrialists are not known in the market and the State Financial Corporations do not get reliable information regarding their business integrity.[8]

On their side the borrowers are unaware of the functions of the

[4] First Annual Report and Accounts, Punjab Financial Corporation, 1954.
[5] Ibid.
[6] First Second and Third Annual Reports, 1954-55-56, Punjab Financial Corporation.
[7] First Annual Report and Accounts, Punjab Financial Corporation, 1954.
[8] Background Papers, Seminar on Financing of Small-Scale Industries in India, Reserve Bank of India, July 1959.

State Financial Corporations and hence do not approach them for credit. Sometimes small-industrialists consider the rate of interest charged by the Corporations high and do not take loans from them. Due to the poverty of many of them small industrialists in some cases cannot afford the expense involved in seeking the services of auditors and accountants to fill up the application forms with the elaborate information required. The State Financial Corporations having no network of branches are inaccessible to many industrialists who might borrow from them if they could reach them easily.[9]

But a review of operations of the Punjab Financial Corporation over a series of years, however, shows a decline in the proportion of applications rejected to applications sanctioned as revealed by statistics. The trends of applications indicate either an improvement in the position of industries seeking loans from the Corporation or a more liberal policy on the part of the Corporation.

A similar trend is noticeable in the Assam Financial Corporation.[10] As in the case of the Punjab Financial Corporation more applications were sanctioned than rejected each year indicating a rapid improvement in the creditworthiness of applicants who approached the Corporation for financial assistance.

On the other hand, in the case of the Uttar Pradesh Financial Corporation the applications rejected exceeded those sanctioned except for the year, 1958-59.[11] This may be taken as an index of a low degree of creditworthiness of applicants in the area under the jurisdiction of the Corporation. In the case of the erstwhile Hyderabad State Financial Corporation, a more or less similar trend was evident.[12] Figures for subsequent years are not available to study the trend of applications in the case of the Andhra Pradesh State Financial Corporation.

The Madhya Pradesh Financial Corporation shows a fluctuating proportion in the applications rejected to those sanctioned.[13] Reasons given by the Corporation for the rejection of applications

---

[9] *Agenda Papers*, Seminar on Financing of Small-Scale Industries in India, Reserve Bank of India, July 1959.

[10] *Fifth Annual Report and Accounts*, Assam Financial Corporation, 1959.

[11] *Fourth Annual Report and Accounts*, Uttar Pradesh Financial Corporation, 1959.

[12] *Second Annual Report*, Hyderabad State Financial Corporation, 1955-56.

[13] *Third and Fourth Annual Reports*, Madhya Pradesh Financial Corporation, 1958-59.

were : inadequate information, improper maintenance of accounts, legal complications, unsatisfactory financial position, unsatisfactory working of the concerns in the past, demand for working capital and loans to reimburse expenditure incurred already, insufficient security, doubtful title of the applicant to the assets offered as security and marketability.[14]

The Orissa State Financial Corporation has registered no change in the two years of its existence.[15] In both the years the ratio of applications rejected to applications sanctioned was 2:1 and the amounts sanctioned and rejected were unchanged. The rejections were due to the uneconomic nature of the schemes presented by the applicants, inadequate information regarding the programme of the parties, insufficient security, inadequate earning capacity and the consequent inability to repay the principal and interest on the loans, unfavourable credit reports, incompetence of the Corporation to lend as the parties were outside the purview of the Corporation's functions and request for working capital.[16]

When applications for loans are not rejected by the State Financial Corporations, sometimes they are kept pending for sanction and disbursement. The delay is due to several causes : very often, after sanction the funds for disbursement are withheld because of defective title to property belonging to the applicant. As mortgagee, a Corporation has to be clear about the legal position in regard to the ownership of assets by the intending borrower in its own interest. For example, when the title to the land on which the factory stands or is to be built is not clear, to rectify the defect, additional documents have to be drawn up and executed to regularize the position which takes time. Sometimes the properties pledged are not in the name of the borrowing concern but the personal names of partners or others. In such cases, the Corporation, to safeguard its own position against bad debts, has to make the partners or others parties to the mortgage deed which again involves some delay in finalizing the loan transaction. There have been instances where essential documents are either missing or have not been executed at all.[17] At times delay is unavoidable : when loans are

---

[14] Ibid.

[15] First and Second Annaul Reports, Orissa Financial Corporation, 1958-59.

[16] First Annual Report and Accounts, Orissa Financial Corporation, 1958.

[17] First and Second Annual Reports, Punjab Financial Corporation, 1954-55.

taken on the mortgage of properties, title-deeds have to be examined with care and various legal formalities gone through resulting in inevitable delay. On vital matters bearing on the loan, some concerns do not furnish full particulars in their applications. They have, therefore, to be interrogated to elicit the needed information.[18] The scrutiny of applications involves time. Various aspects of the borrowing concern call for close examination. Besides the value of the assets offered as security, the earning capacity of the concern needs to be assessed taking into account the efficiency of its plant and machinery, the soundness of the management, availability of raw materials and the like for successful production. This obviously cannot be done in a hurry. The delay is prolonged by the applicants giving insufficient information to a Corporation and the consequent need for reminders to send the necessary particulars.[19] Sometimes the applicants fail to comply with formalities and until they do so, they cannot get the loan.

Once loans are disbursed, sometimes the State Financial Corporations cannot recover them due to defaults on the part of their debtor-concerns. Such defaults may be in respect of repayment of instalments of the principal or interest or both.[20] It is, however, good to know that over certain years there have been no defaults as reported by some State Financial Corporations[21] and in some cases, payment in full has been made even before the due date. But where defaults have occurred, it is heartening to learn that they have been insignificant in some cases.[22]

Among the causes of defaults, financial stringency, change of management or ownership, set-back in business are some important ones, accounting for delay or failure to discharge the debt.[23]

As far as possible, the State Financial Corporations explore every avenue to recover the loans by persuasion. Only as a last resort, they have recourse to compulsion if the other methods prove

[18] *Third Annual Report and Accounts*, Punjab Financial Corporation, 1956.

[19] *Chairman's Speech*, 3rd Annual General Meeting, 1958, Madhya Pradesh Financial Corporation.

[20] *Second and Third Annual Reports*, Bombay Financial Corporation, 1958-59.

[21] *Second Annual Report*, Orissa State Financial Corporation, 1959. *Third and Fourth Annual Reports*, Madhya Pradesh Financial Corporation, 1958-59.

[22] *Fourth, Fifth and Sixth Annual Reports*, Punjab Financial Corporation, 1957-58-59.

[23] *Sixth Annual Report and Accounts*, Kerala Financial Corporation, 1959.

to be ineffective. From an account of the various methods used for the recovery of land, it is evident that a Corporation leaves no stone unturned to make borrowers pay back their loans voluntarily or compulsorily.

Some relief from the burden of debt is provided by a few of the State Financial Corporations through a reduction or exemption of stamp duty. In due course, more State Financial Corporations may provide the concession to their clients if they succeed in their negotiations with the State Governments, for the sanction of such exemption in respect of their mortgage loans to borrowers. The incidence of the duty being heavy, its partial or total exemption will be a source of relief to debtors.[24]

The State Financial Corporations are, however, unable to lower their rates of interest on loans due to the heavy incidence of income-tax and corporation tax.[25] There is a general desire on the part of the State Financial Corporations for relief from these taxes, at least for an initial period of five years to begin with. If the tax burden of the Corporations could be lightened, they could reduce their rate of interest and thereby the burden of debt on the ultimate borrowers. This might lessen the incidence of defaults and overdues.

The State Financial Corporations as shown in the study, give loans to a wide variety of small-scale industries. The large majority of them are consumer goods industries and only a few, producer goods industries.[26] This is significant as showing the predominance of the former group over the latter in the small-scale industrial sector in claiming the attention of the Corporations. It is, further, an index of the under-developed nature of the Indian economy wherein consumer goods take precedence over capital goods.

The Kerala Financial Corporation stands out among the State Financial Corporations followed by the Punjab, Bombay, Bihar, Andhra Pradesh and Uttar Pradesh State Financial Corporations in the matter of amounts advanced to small-scale units. The remaining six Corporations come far behind the above ones.[27]

A striking feature observable in the credit of the Corporations to small-scale units is the disparity in the loans sanctioned and advanced

[24] *First Annual Report and Accounts*, Punjab Financial Corporation, 1954.
[25] *Second Annual Report and Accounts*, Punjab Financial Corporation, 1955.
[26] See Appendix F.
[27] See Appendix G.

by the various State Financial Corporations.[28] Various reasons account for such disparity between loans sanctioned and granted by the State Financial Corporations. When a Corporation sanctions a loan to an applicant, the borrowing concern does not require the entire amount sanctioned all at once. As its obligations mature, it may avail itself of the loan by taking in instalments as and when necessary small portions of the loan. This is done to save interest as far as possible to keep down the cost of borrowed capital incurred by it. When buying assets like land, buildings and machinery, a concern may do so after the sanction of the loan. Since it takes time to finalize the transactions involved in the acquisition of assets, the borrower again takes the loan gradually as he needs. There is, thus, a time-lag between the sanction and the grant or utilization of the credit by a borrower. Some delay in disbursement is also due to the registration of the industrial concerns and taking of licence under the Industries (Development and Regulations) Act, 1951. On its part a Corporation prefers to release a loan in instalments, instead of a lump sum to prevent misuse of funds. By gradual disbursement of funds it ensures their use by the borrower for the specific schemes and purposes they are intended for. For example, when a loan is meant for the purchase of machinery, it is disbursed on the arrival of the shipments; when a building to house a factory is under construction, it is disbursed when the cost is actually incurred. Sometimes, the loan sanctioned has to be reduced, when the value of the assets, according to the report of the assessor, turns out to be less than the value shown by the applicant originally.[29] In some cases, loans are declined after sanction. In others, there may be no clear title to the security offered and loans necessarily lapse. If loans are sought for the purchase of machinery and if it is not available, loans sanctioned may not be given. Pending necessary information and settlement of terms and conditions with the parties concerned, loans granted fall short of loans sanctioned. Non-receipt of requisite import licence has also come in the way of disbursement after sanction.[30] Applicants

[28] See Appendix H.

[29] *First Annual Report and Accounts*, Punjab Financial Corporation, 1954. *First Annual Report and Accounts*, Andhra Pradesh Financial Corporation, 1956-57.

[30] Chairman's Speech, Fourth Annual General Meeting, 1959, Rajasthan Financial Corporation.

postpone or abandon their schemes after the loan has been sanctioned due to loss of interest in the scheme or other reasons. Quite often, applicants are unwilling to trust a Corporation with full information on vital matters and they do not like to be closely examined by officers of the Corporation, or their affairs being scrutinized by them.[31] There is a good deal of delay in completing the necessary formalities regarding mortgage of properties. The applicants at times fail to comply with the conditions imposed on them by a Corporation in order to safeguard its own interests.[32]

Except for the Andhra Pradesh and Rajasthan State Financial Corporations, no State Financial Corporation gave more than a fifth or so of loans of Rs. 50,000 and less. This might be interpreted to imply that small loans do not seem to be popular with most of the State Financial Corporations or there is no demand for them. In the states where Industries and Commerce Department of the Government provides loans up to a limit, as in the case of West Bengal, Kerala and Bombay, the State Financial Corporations do not entertain applications for loans up to those limits to avoid overlapping.[33] However, if small loans are desired for working capital but not forthcoming from the State Financial Corporations, the small-scale industries must be handicapped to some extent for want of working capital. If this is so a change in the policy of the concerned State Financial Corporations in favour of small loans is indicated even if this should involve some administrative inconvenience in the way of book-keeping and debt management.

[31] *First Annual Report and Accounts*, Andhra Pradesh Financial Corporation, 1956-57.

[32] *Second Annual Report and Accounts*, Andhra Pradesh Financial Corporation, 1957-58.

[33] *Background Papers* 3, Seminar on Financing of Small-Scale Industries in India, Reserve Bank of India, July 1959.

CHAPTER IV

THE STATE BANK OF INDIA AND SMALL-SCALE INDUSTRIES

The Pilot Scheme

IN India there are various institutions which may finance small-scale industry, such as the government, the State Financial Corporations, co-operative banks, commercial banks and the State Bank of India. But these sources have not been fully tapped. There is much scope for development of institutional credit which can profitably replace the loans of moneylenders which are notoriously expensive bearing, as they do, usurious rates of interest.

For the promotion of cheap credit from the various organizations to small-scale industry, it is necessary to co-ordinate them besides increasing to the utmost the facilities available from each source. Different institutions supply different kinds of credit, short-term, medium-term and long-term. They can be complementary to each other in meeting the different credit-needs of borrowers who require capital for investment, for varying terms. The government in each state can provide long-term as well as short-term loans under the State Aid to Industries Acts, the Financial Corporations, medium-term capital while the State Bank of India can meet the demand for working capital in the form of short-term loans. Therefore, the different kinds of credit should be integrated into a well-organized system and the various agencies dealing in such credit, made easily accessible to the borrower. To this end, the State Bank of India launched its Pilot Scheme by way of experiment.[1]

The State Bank of India undertook the Pilot Scheme to help small-scale units in getting credit at lower rates of interest than from moneylenders. For the purpose of the scheme, a small-scale industry is interpreted to mean all units which are bigger than cottage industries and handicrafts and smaller than large-scale and medium-scale industries. Further, a small industry is one with capital assets up to Rs. 5,00,000 and employing 50 workers with the use of power, and 100 workers without the use of power. In the light of these

[1] *Advances to Small-Scale Industries*: *Pilot Scheme*, State Bank of India, Central Office, Bombay, 1958.

definitions of small-scale industries, the Pilot Scheme was designed to cover all productive units which particularly answer to such a description and fall within the range of such units. Various agencies are associated with the Pilot Scheme to meet the different credit-needs of small-scale producers. For example, the State Bank of India, the Industries Department of State Governments, the State Financial Corporations and the Small Industries Service Institutes of Government of India are associated with the Pilot Scheme.

The State Bank of India grants short-term loans for working capital; the Industries Departments of State Governments, short-term and long-term loans for small amounts on the security of fixed assets under the State Aid to Industries Acts; and the State Financial Corporations, medium-term loans of fairly large amounts on the security of fixed assets. The Small Industries Service Institute provides technical advice to small-scale industry and recommends it for loans to the National Small Industries Corporation (Private) Ltd. for the purchase of machinery on a hire-purchase basis. The Institute also helps small-scale units in selling their products. It carries out economic surveys of small industries in order to gather requisite data.

To co-ordinate the working of the various agencies which are associated with the Pilot Scheme, there are numerous bodies, viz., the Local Working Party, the Local Co-ordination Committee and the Central Co-ordination Committee which comprise the administrative machinery of the Pilot Scheme.

To obviate going to several agencies for different kinds of credit needed by him the borrower is permitted to submit one application to the Agent of the State Bank of India which fully states his credit needs. On the basis of the application, he is assisted by the State Bank to fill in the application of the concerned agency which has to meet his demand. In case an application is turned down by an agency, it is forwarded to the Small Industries Service Institute to find out if the unit asking for the loans can become eligible for it with technical or organizational improvement. If any applicant should directly approach an agency, the agency will inform the State Bank of the disposal of the application and the action taken.

Under the Pilot Scheme of the State Bank of India, the Bank has to follow a liberal policy in granting credit to small-scale industries. If the bank should adopt its normal policy, many of the small-scale industries would fail to qualify for loans. Very often, they lack acceptable security against which the bank normally gives loans. Sometimes, small industries desiring loans may be technically and/ or organizationally unsound and hence must go disappointed. To meet such cases, the State Bank has liberalized its rules and relaxed some of its conditions for the grant of loans. Further, to help those intending borrowers who fall short of the requirements, being found wanting in technical and/or organizational competence, a programme of improvement has been introduced under which deficient units undergo technical and/or organizational improvements so as to become eligible for credit from the various agencies which offer it to them. By these means it is sought to cover as many units as possible to render help to small-scale industry even though many of them may not be up to the mark. However, the lending agency can minimize the risk by advancing credit to borrowers who produce marketable goods. On the strength of marketability, loans may be given when no other normal safeguards are available.

Under agreements with the State Financial Corporations, the services of the Bank are placed at their disposal in the matter of collecting reports on parties, processing applications and disbursing loans to the borrowers. The wide net-work of branches which the Bank possesses can be used by the Corporations which have a limited number of offices of their own, in giving loans to borrowers, scattered far and wide.

The Pilot Scheme aimed at joint action by different institutions to meet the financial and other needs of small-scale industries. Under it, the applicant may apply to one agency for short-term, medium-term or long-term loans. Since various agencies participate in the Pilot Scheme, loan applications are examined by them jointly. The State Bank of India, the State Financial Corporation, the co-operative bank and the Director of Industries consult each other in disposing of applications. Loans are sanctioned by the appropriate agency, either by itself or in collaboration with others when the borrower needs more than one kind of credit.

Under the Pilot Scheme the State Bank of India adopted a liberal policy in order to extend greater facilities of credit to borrowers. When the scheme first came into being in April 1956, the procedure followed in granting credit was more rigid. But it was realized subsequently that the Pilot Scheme could become effective only if the different agencies involved offered their assistance more freely through a liberal loan policy. The State Bank of India soon took steps to do so. The range of raw materials which could serve as. security for loans was widened to include any raw material which was used in making a marketable commodity. To extend liberalized credit over a larger area, the Pilot Scheme has been extended to all the branches of the Bank, since the beginning of 1959, so that no small-scale industry is beyond the reach of the Bank's Pilot Scheme wherever branches of the Bank operate.[2]

A few case studies of liberalized credit offered by the State Bank of India reveal how the loan policy of the Bank under its Pilot Scheme works in practice. One company manufacturing metal safes, boxes, etc. came into being in 1942. But for the Pilot Scheme and the liberal policy which the State Bank came to follow under it, the industry would have been denied any credit. If the proprietor mortgaged his fixed assets, as he intended to do, he would have no unencumbered assets, in the result, the Bank would not have ordinarily accommodated the concern. The products of the industry, despite their great popularity sold in a restricted market, being of a specialized nature and lack of marketability would have normally stood in the way of the Bank in lending to the industry. And yet, owing to the new terms of credit evolved by the Bank, due weight was given to the technical ability, the business integrity and the gratifying record of the industry in the past. The installed capacity of the factory expanded and production went up together with the quality of the goods. The industry's products gained in marketability and led to an increased demand for working capital. The Bank gave working capital up to Rs. 2 lakhs in successive stages to meet the growing needs of the industry.

Although finance was forthcoming, there was a shortage of essential raw materials like iron and steel which the industry needed for its production. If they were available, the industry might have done even better.[3] This shows how important non-financial factors such as abundant raw materials are, and how their lack can be a drag on an industry's progress.

Another case concerns a company which. was granted a cash credit to the extent of Rs. 30,000, on the security of its raw materials

---

[2] *Case Studies in Small Industries Finance*, State Bank of India, May 1959.
[3] *Ibid.*

(mild steel items) and finished products (nuts, bolts, screws, pipe fittings, etc.), to be kept under the Bank's lock and key. The client being new to the Bank, it asked for a guarantee to safeguard its own position. This the applicant was unable to produce.

It is significant that the Bank went out of its way to help a needy producer who lacked adequate security in the shape of raw materials for a demand cash-credit and a suitable guarantee for a clean advance in the absence of such security. This instance may serve as an index of the new policy of the State Bank in regard to industrial finance in the sphere of small-scale industries. The case is also noteworthy for the sympathetic attitude of the State Bank to a totally new client with whom the Bank had had no business dealings before. A way out was found when all normal channels were closed to help the applicant with usual forms of credit like demand cash-credit or a clean advance against a proper guarantee. With the assistance of the Bank, the firm which had incurred losses in 1955-6 began to earn profits in 1957 which increased in 1958 showing that the Bank's credit was being well used by the borrower. But for the help rendered by the Bank, the firm might well have continued to make losses and perhaps eventually been closed down. It goes to the credit of the Bank that it took a risk in propping up a losing concern and put it on its feet. It indicates, further, that if commercial banks similarly took some risk and were bolder, even industries which were backward and losing might acquit themselves well in the end and prove worthy clients. The experience of the State Bank of India in this instance has a moral for all commercial banks, not to say for the State Bank itself, to abandon an over-cautious loan policy and be more venturesome in offering credit to ambitious entrepreneurs in need of finance.

The case studies reveal that the Bank considered each applicant on his individual merits and went to his aid. If it had applied general principles to all cases alike, none of the applicants might have satisfied the Bank. If the foregoing cases are random samples, their treatment by the Bank points to a careful individual attention bestowed by it on each applicant and its sympathetic disposal of each case. All the cases cited have succeeded in getting credit from the Bank. It would be instructive to know of a few cases of borrowers who have failed to do so in spite of the Bank's sincere efforts to oblige them. Such case studies might reveal the limits beyond which the Bank cannot go even with the best intentions to help them. The Bank may well consider publishing a few cases of this kind for the benefit of the public. A knowledge of such cases will also evoke an appreciative understanding on the part of the public of the Bank's genuine inability to help utterly non-creditworthy applicants who ask for loans.

The loans disbursed were given to a variety of small-scale industries. Among them the engineering industry was most prominent.

The State Bank of India reviewed the progress of the Pilot Scheme from its inception in April 1956 to the end of December 1957. The Evaluation Team covered the 9 centres where the Pilot Scheme was first introduced. It was intended to assess the progress of the scheme; investigate to what extent the decisions of the State Bank of India, under its liberalized policy of credit to small-scale industries, were being carried out; study the effect of the methods and procedures of financial institutions on small-scale industries; discover the shortcomings of the scheme and learn to improve it, on the basis of past experience of its working; and modify the Bank's policy to make the scheme more effective in the future.[4]

The survey revealed that the progress of the scheme varied from centre to centre. Although no striking progress was evident anywhere, the scheme was fairly successful and justified itself.

Normally, only 13 of the 123 applications sanctioned would have been eligible for credit under the State Bank's rules, but, owing to the liberal terms under the Pilot Scheme, the Bank was able to sanction credit to 110 more applicants. This is significant as an index of the new trends in the lending policies of the State Bank of India. It is, further, noteworthy that the 133 applicants who were sanctioned loans were granted credit on security other than raw materials. The average rate of interest was $5\frac{1}{4}$ per cent, exclusive of small charges for the salaries of godown-keepers and watchmen.

Of the 32 small-scale industrial units interviewed by the Evaluation Team, 30 reported an increase in production as a result of the credit facilities received under the Pilot Scheme. During the period under review, it was found that there were no bad debts in any of the 9 centres covered for purposes of evaluation. Of the small-scale industries financed in the nine centres by the State Bank of

---

[4] *Background Papers* 4, Seminar on Financing of Small-Scale Industries in India, Reserve Bank of India, July 1959.

India, under its Pilot Scheme, the majority were engineering and metal industries.[5]

As pointed out above, the progress of the Pilot Scheme was not uniform at the various centres so that only some centres had a better record of work to their credit. This was attributable not so much to the fact that, where progress was greater, the small-scale industries seeking credit were better suited for accommodation as to the fact of greater initiative and sympathy of the Bank staff in helping them. It would appear, therefore, that a progressive and helpful attitude is an important factor in promoting institutional credit in the sector of small-scale industries.

On the basis of its findings, the Evaluation Team made various recommendations: encouraged by the success of the scheme, it was suggested that the scheme be extended to all branches of the State Bank. To facilitate greater borrowing by small-scale units from the Bank, it was suggested that the list of acceptable commodities serving as security for loans be enlarged. To make the credit cheaper, it was suggested that the maximum rate of interest be 6 per cent, inclusive of all charges, like godown-keepers' salaries, watchmen's salaries, inspection charges. The Bank should consider fixed asset in the form of machinery as security for short-term loans. The Team recommended, in the interests of greater co-ordination between various agencies financing small-scale industries, that State Governments should route their loans through the State Financial Corporations to the small-scale units. It further recommended that the State Financial Corporations "enter into an agreement with the State Bank of India to act as their agents for collecting reports, disbursing loans, collecting instalments from small-scale industries."

Accordingly, the State Bank has since implemented some of the recommendations of the Evaluation Team. The scheme was extended to all branches of the Bank with effect from 1 January 1959. However, at certain important centres, the scheme will be more intensively worked and at those places, since other financing agencies, governmental and private, were operating, it is intended to lend to small-scale industries in co-ordination with such agencies to the maximum extent possible. The Bank has enlarged its list of accept-

[5] B. P. Patel, "Financing of Small-Scale Industries," *The Journal of the Indian Institute of Bankers*, April 1959, Vol. XXX, No. 2.

able commodities against which it will give loans. This is safe as the range of marketable industrial goods produced in the country has increased and can serve as security for loans.[6] The Bank has accepted the recommendation to fix the maximum rate of interest at 6 per cent per annum, inclusive of all charges. To facilitate modernization of small-scale units, their expansion or renovation, the Bank has decided to grant medium-term loans to eligible applicants for periods up to 7 years against suitable security.[7] To bring about the necessary psychological change in the attitudes and outlook of the staff, the Bank is taking steps to impart the requisite training to foster initiative and sympathy in them in handling small-scale industrialists.[8]

[6] *Background Papers* 4, Seminar on Financing of Small-Scale Industries in India, Reserve Bank of India, July 1959.

[7] B. P. Patel, "Financing of Small-Scale Industries," *The Journal of the Indian Institute of Bankers*, April 1959, Vol. XXX, No. 2.

[8] *Ibid.*

CHAPTER V

OTHER COMMERCIAL BANKS AND SMALL-SCALE INDUSTRIES

Scheduled and Non-Scheduled Banks

AMONG the institutional sources of credit, commercial banks in India finance small-scale industries to some extent. To estimate the amount of credit given by them to small-scale and medium-scale industries, the Reserve Bank of India made a sample survey of advances by scheduled and non-scheduled banks to such industries.[1]

Of the total advances by banks to small-scale industries over 94 per cent were given by scheduled banks and less than 6 per cent by non-scheduled banks. This indicates the insignificant position of non-scheduled banks *vis a vis* the scheduled banks. However, over 80 per cent of the total advances of non-scheduled banks in the country was in the three southern states of Kerala, Madras and Mysore. Of the three states, Kerala alone claimed about half of the total credit given. The large share of the three states was due to the concentration of non-scheduled banks in these States.[2]

The bulk of the credit (78 per cent) was given to trade and next to trade, industry claimed 18 per cent of the total amount. In the sphere of trade 85 per cent of the advances was to the non-corporate sector.[3] But in the sphere of industry the corporate and non-corporate sectors had more or less equal proportions of credit.

As on 30 September 1957, the Reserve Bank survey revealed that small-scale units in some industries enjoyed a substantial share of bank advances. Thus, small-scale units in the iron and steel and light engineering industries received Rs. 4.3 crores of the total loans. Similarly, in oil-crushing the proportion of credit to small-scale units was fairly large.[4]

Of the various forms of security, finished goods and raw materials seem to be least popular with banks. On the other hand, stock-in-trade, documentary bills and government securities, shares and bonds were more acceptable to banks.

[1] *Background Papers* 6, Seminar on Financing of Small-Scale Industries in India, Reserve Bank of India, July 1959.
[2] *Ibid.*   [3] *Ibid.*   [4] *Ibid.*

47

Broadly, the survey revealed that scheduled banks played a more important part in financing small-scale and medium-scale industries than it was realized. But the bulk of their credit was given to trade and only about 12 per cent of it to industry. There was need for increasing their credit to industry.

But according to the earlier surveys of the Reserve Bank of India, banks played a comparatively less significant role in financing small-scale industries. According to the 1952 survey of the Reserve Bank of India, the scheduled banks had lent only 10.8 per cent of their total industrial advances to small-scale concerns.[5] Since then, there has been an improvement. As noted earlier, the scheduled banks, as on 30 September 1957, made over 30 per cent of their loans to small-scale industries. Credit from the scheduled banks had thus increased by 300 per cent in half a decade, from 1952-57.

Further, surveys of individual industries revealed the small share of commercial banks in the finances of the industries. Compared to the other sources, the commercial banks played the least important part.[6]

But according to the Reserve Bank survey which revealed the position as on 30 September 1957, light engineering industry was among the small-scale industries which received a substantial part of commercial bank credit. Both the general trend in small-scale industries as a whole and the trend in individual industries seem to be encouraging, indicating an increase in commercial bank finance of small-scale firms.

Although the trends of commercial bank credit reveal an increase, it is estimated that of the total commercial bank credit, only 10 per cent goes to the small-scale sector in the country and on the whole the banks play a minor role in this sector.[7]

By comparison, commercial banks in some of the other countries of the world such as Japan, U. S. A., Sweden and Switzerland lend more to small-scale industries. In Japan, as on 30 June 1958, local banks granted 55 per cent of their loans to small business and the city banks, 25 per cent. The loans of the local banks and

[5] C. K. Shah, "Commercial Banks and Finance for Small Industries in India," *The Journal of the Indian Institution of Bankers*, October 1957.

[6] *Ibid.*

[7] *Agenda Papers* II (*b*), Seminar on Financing of Small-Scale Industries in India, Reserve Bank of India, July 1959.

city banks amounted to 54 per cent of the loans granted to small business by all financial institutions.[8] In the U. S. A., commercial banks make 20 per cent of their loans to small business and the smaller banks, in particular, about 80 per cent.[9] In Sweden, commercial banks finance small-scale industries to a large extent. In 1953, they had given loans to small-scale units amounting to 35 per cent of their total credit to industry and trade. And one of the largest commercial banks, AB Svenska Handels Banken had given 28 per cent of its industrial credit to small industry.[10] In Switzerland, where there are no special institutions to finance small enterprises, the local banks numbering 365 (as at the end of 1952) cater for the needs of small trades and handicrafts.[11]

Some of the causes of the low percentage of commercial bank credit to small-scale industries in India could be found in the various failings of small producers, discovered in our study of the State Financial Corporations : lack of managerial ability, technical skill, proper accounts, full information on their production and markets. Further, the applicants from the small-scale industrial sector do not offer suitable security to the banks for short-term loans. Owing to lack of statistical and other relevant information on the industries in question, their prospects of earning profits and repaying the loans cannot be assessed with any measure of certainty. Hence, it is considered highly risky to lend to these industries. According to the Shroff Committee, many small banks which had lent heavily to small units failed in some areas and banks have since generally avoided lending to them.[12] Moreover, large banks invest their funds mostly in more secure large-scale industries than in small-scale ones. Small banks, apart from their reluctance to lend to small producers, lack funds.[13]

[8] *Background Papers* 13, Seminar on Financing of Small-Scale Industries in India, Reserve Bank of India, July 1959.

[9] *Agenda Papers* II (*b*), Seminar on Financing of Small-Scale Industries in India, Reserve Bank of India, July 1959.

[10] *Report on Small Industries in India*, Ford Foundation Team, 1955.

[11] *Background Papers* 12, Seminar on Financing of Small-Scale Industries in India, Reserve Bank of India, July 1959.

[12] *Capital for Medium and Small-Scale Industries*, Society for Social and Economic Studies, 1959.

[13] *Background Papers* 6, Seminar on Financing of Small-Scale Industries in India, Reserve Bank of India, July 1959.

On their side, banks in India suffer from various handicaps unlike their counterparts in some countries abroad. They lack credit bureaux to furnish information regarding their clients. To safeguard their resources against default, credit guarantee and insurance are absent by and large. A beginning, however, is being made, in this matter : the National Small Industries Corporation guarantees advances against raw materials granted by the State Bank of India to small-scale industries executing government contracts. It, however, touches only the fringe of the problem. The Reserve Bank of India has introduced, from 1960, a guarantee scheme for bank-loans to small-scale industries.[14] In India adequate or reliable statistical data are not available to banks regarding the installed capacity, production, extent of demand and so on and banks are unable to assess the present condition and future prospects of small-scale producers and small producers do not disclose all the facts required by banks. The system of participation loans has not been developed in this country which might have encouraged banks to venture into the small-scale sector as in the U.S.A.[15]

If, therefore, the creditworthiness of small-scale industrialists is improved and the various handicaps of the bankers are removed, banks will make no discrimination against small producers as against large ones, according to leading bankers.[16]

The creditworthiness of small-scale industrialists would depend on non-financial aids to improve their condition, technically and commercially, so as to make them eligible for institutional credit in general and commercial bank credit in particular.

To remove the handicaps which now hamper commercial banks in lending to small producers, it would be necessary to create credit information bureaux in the country, promote credit guarantee and insurance to protect banks against loss, collect accurate and sufficient statistics for the benefit of lending institutions in order to investigate the requirements and repaying capacity of borrowers.

It is by such positive measures that banks must be encouraged to lend to small-scale industries and not by relaxing the terms and conditions of loans at the expense of their depositors.

---

[14] *The Hindu*, 5 November 1959, Reserve Bank of India, Press Communique.
[15] *Agenda Papers* II (*b*), Seminar on Financing of Small-Scale Industries in India, Reserve Bank of India, July 1959.
[16] *Ibid.*

At present, the government, through various organizations, such as the National Small Industries Corporation, Small Industries Service Institutes, industrial estates, is rendering assistance to small-scale industries to improve their condition. These efforts may well be supplemented by banks and other financial institutions in the country, financing small-scale industries. In the U.S.A. and Japan, the State, the financial institutions and the business community jointly try to solve the financial as well as the non-financial problems of small business.[17] In the long run, such a course of action in India will be necessary as the State will not be able to cope with the problem. The commercial banks, the State Financial Corporations, the Chambers of Commerce and the Small-Scale Industries Board could all share the responsibility which has now devolved entirely on the Small-Scale Industries Board representing the State.

In America and Japan, with the all-round improvement of small business, banks have been able to finance them in a large measure.[18] Even so, if small-scale industries in India are improved, they will inspire confidence in the banks and attract more loans.

It has been suggested that small-scale industries should receive a favoured treatment from banks. For example, they should be charged a lower rate of interest. But, on account of the greater risk involved in lending to them and the higher costs of administration as a result of the complicated procedure for small loans, it may not be possible to offer a concession to them. A bank, which is a profit-making organization and has to pay interest to depositors and dividends to shareholders, cannot charge less to small producers. If it is subsidized by the State, it might be able to do so.[19] Although such a concession is not offered by banks in other countries like Japan and the U.S.A.[20] to small businesses, in India such a concession should be offered in the initial stages with the financial assistance of the State because commercial banks provide a small proportion of their credit to small-scale industries and there is great need of developing institutional credit in the country to wean away small-scale industries from non-institutional sources, money-lenders, who leave much to be desired. Later, when the industries get stronger, the concession could be withdrawn.

The suggestion to lower the standards of the banks to accommodate small-scale industries is fraught with grave danger to the banks

[17] *Ibid.*   [18] *Ibid.*   [19] *Ibid.*   [20] *Ibid.*

themselves and the borrowers. The banks can ill-afford to do so as trustees of depositors' savings, kept in their custody for safe-keeping. Such a relaxation is apt to demoralize the borrowers. It is noteworthy that in Japan and the U.S.A., applications of small businesses are screened like those of large ones. The criteria for lending are the same for all. Misguided sympathy will do more harm than good to small producers. What is required is the raising of the standards of producers to the necessary level so as to make them eligible clients. To this end, they have to be educated in every way, technically, organizationally and even morally, to promote business integrity and efficiency which are at a woefully low ebb among them. In the U.S.A., banks, through their associations, have taken steps, with the help of other organizations and the State, to educate and improve the small businessmen.[21] But in India commerical banks have remained aloof from small-scale industries. In view of their growing importance, in the planned economic development of the country, in their own interest, banks should make efforts to explore this field which may prove very profitable even to themselves.

With an improvement in management and technical efficiency, marketing and business integrity of small-scale industries, banks in India may be able to evolve new forms of loans and advances to them in keeping with the genius of the country even as banks in the U.S.A. have made several innovations like term-loans for working capital and capital expenditure, instalment loans, loans on the security of real estate and accounts-receivable[22] and so on.

As in Japan, banks in India should perform agency functions for a commission for other financial institutions, like the State Financial Corporations and the Government. This would give them an insight into the nature of financing small-scale industries and encourage them to undertake such financing on their own.

In the U.S.A., commercial banks, in the years of the Second World War, gave a major part of their credit to medium and small business units as a result of the central guaranteeing system instituted in 1942 (Regulation V Programme of the Federal Reserve System). With the end of the War and the termination of the Regulation V programme, the Reconstruction Finance Corporation introduced its blanket guarantee scheme in 1945 to guarantee commercial bank loans. As a result of it, the volume of loans in 1945 and 1946

[21] *Ibid.*   [22] *Ibid.*

increased. The scheme was terminated in 1947. In its place the Reconstruction Finance Corporation introduced a "Small Loans Participation Plan" to guarantee loans. During the Korean War, in 1950, the Regulation V Programme was revived. Thus, both in war and peace, bank loans were guaranteed in the U.S.A.

The system of credit guarantee and insurance, prevalent in Japan since 1937, has facilitated lending by commercial banks to small business.

Even in small countries, loan-guarantee schemes have helped small businesses to secure advances from banks. In Philippines, the Industrial Guarantee and Loan Fund, set up in 1952, has been useful to banks. By the end of 1957, the Fund had given guarantees for 12 industrial loans amounting to £ 5.1 million.[23]

The examples of U.S.A., Japan and other countries may well be copied in India.

In India, the Reserve Bank of India has introduced a guarantee scheme for bank loans to small-scale industries since July 1960.[24] It is to be on an experimental basis for a period of two years to begin with. In the first year, the scheme is to cover 21 districts. The guarantee will apply to credit and overdraft arrangements, demand and term loans to small-scale industries for purposes of working capital or acquisition of fixed assets and equipment. All advances sanctioned by banks to small-scale industrial units will be eligible for guarantee. In the first year, the scheme will cover 300 banks' offices in 57 centres in the 21 districts in addition to apex co-operative banks. In the second year, the scheme will be extended to 21 more districts. The guarantee will be provided by the government through the Reserve Bank of India which is to administer the scheme. At the end of the two years, the working of the scheme will be reviewed to evaluate the results of the scheme. The scheme is the outcome of the deliberations of the Seminar on Financing of Small Scale Industries in India organized by the Reserve Bank of India in July 1959 at Hyderabad. The scheme is intended to protect banks against possible loss in respect of their loans to small-scale industries.

To widen the scope of the scheme, banks other than those selected may also enjoy guarantee facilities if an apex co-operative bank is

[23] *Ibid.*
[24] *The Hindu,* 5 November 1959, Reserve Bank of India, Press Communique.

prepared to participate in the loan up to at least 25 per cent. Although loans given after the scheme comes into operation will be eligible for guarantee, if loans given prior to that date are renewed or enhanced, they may also be guaranteed. In the experimental phase of the scheme, the rate charged will be one-fourth of one per cent per annum on the amount of the advance. The low rate is intended to encourage banks to take advantage of the facility and lend more confidently to small-scale producers. To make the scheme popular and effective the procedure of operation will be quick and simple.

In Netherlands, the guarantee funds in certain branches of industry like the grocery trade, established by more fortunate businessmen to help their deserving colleagues in need of assistance have been useful to small businessmen. Where such funds are not found, the General Guarantee Fund set up by the government in that country comes to the rescue of borrowers. In India the well-to-do small-scale industrialists and even large-scale industries, depending on small-scale industries for stores, might establish similar guarantee funds as a complement to the guarantee scheme contemplated by the State and the Reserve Bank of India.

Small industrialists, owing to poverty and dire need of the moment, sometimes spend credit on consumption expenditure. This presents a serious problem to intending lenders such as credit institutions, as chances of default are increased due to this cause. It is interesting that in Colombia, in Latin America, the Banco Popular (People's Bank) gives loans for consumption on the security of wages and salaries as well as for investment. In India, if some consumption loans were thus made available by special institutions, the incidence of defaults and bad debts could be reduced to some extent. As it is, sometimes co-operative societies allow their borrowers to use borrowed funds for consumption purposes. If the practice were legalized, there would be fewer cases of default on the part of borrowers. If the State were to subsidize the commercial banks, they could perhaps give loans for consumption like the Banco Popular in Colombia. On their own, the banks in India, being orthodox, are likely to resist such a suggestion as dangerous but, with State backing, they may give it a trial and watch the outcome.

There is need of information about small producers. Credit

enquiry agencies as in Japan, to collect and furnish lending banks information on intending borrowers, should be developed. In that country banks depend on such agencies to make decisions on loan-applications. Mutual exchange of information by banks on their clients is also indicated.

CHAPTER VI

CO-OPERATIVE BANKS AND
SMALL-SCALE INDUSTRIES

IN India, among the various institutional sources of credit, since 1904, co-operative banks have been one. The co-operative organization, spread over the whole country, comprises rural and urban banks.

The co-operative organization is a potential source of credit to small-scale industries. Co-operative banks can finance individual industrialists as well as industrial co-operatives. The urban co-operative banks can finance individuals while the Central and State Co-operative Banks, industrial co-operative societies.[1]

Realizing the potentialities of co-operation for the small-scale sector, the government took measures to promote industrial co-operatives under the First Five Year Plan. As a result of these efforts on the part of the Central and State Governments, the number of co-operatives increased as follows:

Date	No. of Industrial Co-operatives
30 June 1951	7,105
,, 1956	15,333
,, 1957	16,746

It will be seen that, during the First Five Year Plan period, the number of industrial co-operatives in the country more than doubled. Industrial co-operatives for small-scale industries, such as light engineering goods, sports goods and furniture were mostly concentrated in the Punjab, Delhi, West Bengal and Bombay.[2]

The co-operative organization, further, offers scope for non-financial assistance to small-scale industries, much of which is now

[1] *Agenda Papers* II (*c*), Seminar on Financing of Small-Scale Industries in India, Reserve Bank of India, July 1959.

[2] *Report of the Working Group on Industrial Co-operatives*, Government of India, 1958.

being provided by the State, through its agencies, like the National Small Industries Corporation, the industrial estates and the Small Industries Service Institutes. In the long run, small-scale industries have to rely more and more on themselves for which purpose they can organize co-operative societies for marketing, production, provision of facilities, etc. Service societies, mentioned above, perform such functions, for their members.

So far, industrial co-operatives have been financed mainly by the government, under the State Aid to Industries Acts, in the various states. While some central co-operative banks have resources to finance industrial co-opratives, they cannot lend at the low rates of interest required by the government because of the high administrative costs and allocations to reserve funds and so on. In common with credit institutions, equipped partly with public deposits, the co-operative banks cannot relax their terms and conditions of credit without endangering their position. They have to base their loan-policies on efficiency of management, bright prospects of sale and profits and economic viability of borrowing industrial co-operatives. Yet another factor impeding co-operative banks from lending to industrial co-operatives is lack of representatives of industrial co-operatives on their boards of management and technical experts on their staff to help them understand their problems and assess their credit requirements. Above all, co-operative banks are predominantly interested in agricultural credit. In the result, they have yet to develop sufficient interest in industrial finance. Owing to the foregoing reasons, co-operative financing agencies have done little in the way of lending to industrial co-operatives.[3]

In a few states in the country such as Bombay, Mysore and Uttar Pradesh, industrial co-operative banks have been set up to finance industrial co-operatives.[4]

Institutional financial agencies have played a minor role in the co-operative sector of small-scale industries as sources of credit. On the other hand, the State has been more prominent in financing industrial co-operatives. But government as a source of credit suffers from numerous shortcomings. Government is a poor substitute for a proper financial institution designed specially to perform banking functions. Owing to the bureaucratic set-up and the inevitable protracted procedures involved, there will be delay due to red-

[3] *Ibid.*   [4] *Ibid.*

tape. Generally, government credit assumes the form of loans but working capital is more convenient in the form of cash-credit. Such limitations prove the inappropriateness of the State as a lending agency. In view of this, it has been suggested that financial institutions take over from the State its financial functions in respect of industrial co-operatives.[5] However, in the short run, at any rate, notwithstanding the various defects in government financing, it appears that it cannot be avoided since financial institutions will not lend to industrial co-operatives in their present state. They need to be strengthened and stabilized first. Such improvement, however, will take time. In the meanwhile, the State alone can continue its assistance to small-scale industries, organized co-operatively or otherwise.

Owing to a variety of reasons, institutional finance is not forthcoming. However, efforts are being made by the government, through different measures, to render small-scale industries creditworthy. But, until they actually can be trusted with loans, it is necessary to protect institutional lenders against defaults. It is a sense of insecurity which has so far stood in the way of their giving credit. If some assurance of repayment by borrowers were made, financial institutions can have no objection to lending them. It is, therefore, suggested that the government, in the short run, should guarantee institutional loans, whenever necessary.[6]

It is, however, gratifying to note that since the publication of the Report of the Working Group on Industrial Co-operatives in July 1958, the State Financial Corporations have financed industrial co-operatives in varying degrees. As in July 1958, only two industrial co-operatives had been financed by the Bombay State Financial Corporation. The other State Financial Corporations had not financed any industrial co-operatives.[7] Since then, the position has slightly improved.

Thus, as envisaged by the Working Group on Industrial Co-operatives, the Co-operative Banks and the State Bank of India should, between them, provide the working capital and the State Governments and the State Financial Corporations, medium and long-term capital to industrial co-operatives.

Since the publication of the Report of the Working Group on Industrial Co-operatives in July 1958, the assistance rendered by

[5] *Ibid.*   [6] *Ibid.*   [7] *Ibid.*

the State Financial Corporations to industrial co-operatives has increased. The State Bank of India has since extended its Pilot Scheme to all its branches. The government, through the Reserve Bank of India, has decided to guarantee loans of commercial banks to small-scale industries. These trends point to greater willingness on the part of financial agencies to finance small-scale industries in the country. In the light of recent experience, the Working Group on Industrial Co-operatives seems to be justified in holding the opinion that the existing agencies could perform the functions of industrial co-operative banks effectively. However, in the long run, if conditions are ripe and a suitable climate for industrial co-operative banks should exist, they may be contemplated. In the short run, it would seem advisable to strengthen the existing co-operative organization and other financial institutions and modify their policies rather than establish new industrial co-operative banks, which may only result in the duplication of banking services.

As in the case of individual entrepreneurs in the small-scale sector, industrial co-operatives also need non-financial aid for their growth and development. The investigations of the Working Group on Industrial Co-operatives have brought to light many handicaps of industrial co-operatives.[8] They are unable to get adequate raw materials of the right quality at fair prices. In consequence of the various difficulties in respect of raw materials, industrial co-operatives prove uneconomic and when they manage to turn out products, they are of inferior quality, which prejudices the public against them. Apart from the general shortage of raw materials which is experienced by industrial co-operatives, the scarcity of some controlled materials, such as iron and steel, cement, coal and coke is specially acute. The Group made various suggestions to help industrial co-operative to get raw materials. The progress of industrial co-operatives has been hampered, further, by lack of technical skill and up-to-date machinery. Yet another handicap of industrial co-operatives is want of proper facilities for marketing their finished products. On account of various drawbacks and difficulties, marketing poses a problem to industrial co-operatives. Apart from providing the marketing machinery, the State could absorb a part of the supply from industrial co-operatives, by purchasing from them what they produce. In this

[8] *Ibid.*

regard, however, only some State Governments in the country patronize specially industrial co-opratives. This was, because, the State Governments were dissatisfied with the quality of their products or did not receive them in time. Sometimes, the instructions to departments of government were not clear and specific. Owing to these reasons, industrial co-operatives did not enjoy the patronage of the State in any special way.

Besides the government, large-scale industries could purchase their components and parts, where possible, from industrial co-operatives which can manufacture them. Under its Government Purchase Division, the Natiolal Small Industries Corporation has procured the bulk of the orders from the government for small-scale units and very little for industrial co-operatives. However, under its Export Section, a part of the orders for foot-wear for export to Russia was executed by leather workers co-operative societies of Uttar Pradesh, Bombay and Madras.

CHAPTER VII

FINANCES FOR SMALL-SCALE
INDUSTRIES ABROAD

SMALL-SCALE industry plays no mean part in the economic activity of several highly industrialized nations, such as Japan and Germany, Switzerland and France, Great Britain and the United States. The way they have solved the problem of finance for their small-scale industries will be of interest to India. We might well learn some lessons from abroad in the present predicament of unemployment and over-population in order to put our own small producers on a sound financial footing.

It will be of special interest to know how the Japanese have tackled the question of finance in regard to their small-scale industry because, since India won her independence, the government has adopted the Japanese model as the basis for the reorganization of Indian small-scale industry.[1] As in India, the problems of small-scale industries in Japan are both financial and non-financial.

The Government of Japan has set up several special institutions to provide medium and long-term credit to small-scale industries. When the various financial institutions fail to meet the demand of small business, the special institutions set up by the government accommodate them.

Yet another feature of Japanese financial organization is the security of credit enjoyed by financial institutions against loss and default of borrowers. For this, there is a system of compensation for loss, credit guarantee and credit insurance in Japan.[2]

In Japan, the credit enquiry agency system is highly developed. The financial institutions use the services of these agencies to get information on the creditworthiness of applicants and take decisions on their loan applications, with the guidance of the agencies. Further, banks also exchange information on their clients.[3]

In Japan, the State has taken various measures to make small-

---

[1] G. M. Laud, *Co-operative Banking in India*, 1956.

[2] *Background Papers* 13, Seminar on Financing of Small-Scale Industries in India, Reserve Bank of India, July 1959.

[3] *Ibid.*

scale industries sound and worthy of assistance. Industries which are weak are helped to become strong and eventually self-reliant. Once they are put on their feet, they carry on.

It is note-worthy that more than half of the smaller industries have organized themselves into co-operative form of business organization in Japan.[4]

Numerically, small enterprises are in the majority in the United States of America. They constitute the bulk of the 2.5 million business units in that country.[5] As elsewhere, small businesses present problems of finance in the United States of America.

It is note-worthy that commercial banks were induced to lend to medium and small concerns and as a result of the central guaranteeing system instituted in 1942 (under regulation V programme of the Federal Reserve System), they were responsible for a major part of the credit to such units. This was largely due to the guarantee plan designed to remove the risk of loss which generally prevented commercial banks lending to small businesses. When such risk was taken over by the guaranteeing agency the resistance of banks disappeared. This is a lesson well worth learning wherever commercial bank credit is not forthcoming, for the small-scale sector, as in India.

To meet the shortage of long-term credit and equity capital in the small business sector, Small Business Investment Companies are to be established, under the Small Business Investment Companies Act of August 1958, in the various States, with a capital stock and reserves of $300,000 in each company. The Small Business Administration, National Banks and State Member Banks are authorized to subscribe to the capital of the companies. The Companies are intended to furnish equity capital and long-term loans to small business concerns. They may take the assistance of commercial banks in the investigation of applications, servicing of loans, etc. for a fee. In India, similar organizations to furnish equity capital are indicated.

As it is well known, the British Joint-Stock Banks, unlike the continental banks like those in Germany, do not finance industry. However, the fact that they hold shares in organizations such as the Industrial and Commercial Finance Coporation points to their indirect participation in industrial finance and their contribution

[4] *Ibid.*   [5] *Ibid.*

to the finances of small-scale industry in the country. In India, similarly, joint-stock banks like the scheduled banks subscribe to the capital of State Financial Corporations which give long-term and medium-term loans to small-scale industry.

There was lack of adequate finance for small enterprises in France. As other sources of credit and capital were not open to them, special institutions were set up. Owing to the development of industrial finance by the German Banks, the large-scale industries are financed by the bigger banks. To cover smaller industries, "trade banks" were opened in the thirties of this century, to supply cheap credit. There are no special institutions to finance small enterprises in Switzerland. The local banks which numbered about 365 at the end of 1952, cater for the needs of small traders and handicrafts. Institutional finance plays an important part in the sector of small-scale industry in Sweden. For financing small industries, in Italy, there are several public organizations. In Netherlands, a guarantee fund is established in each branch of an industry by businessmen, to help deserving colleagues in getting loans for a new venture. Where such funds exist, the government also partly guarantees the loans of the Bank. A guarantee fund exists in the grocery trade and similar funds are being contemplated in other branches of industry. The State has set up a General Guarantee Fund for the trades-people who do not have the advantage of a guarantee fund, in their lines of business.

In Finland, there is no special agency to finance small industry. The State helps it through the channel of local, commercial and co-operative banks. The loans given by the government are disbursed and recovered by them.

There are some special organizations in Belgium to finance small enterprises.

In Burma there is a similarity with India in regard to State aid. In Burma, too, similar steps have been taken to finance and assist small-scale industries by means of government loans, hire-purchase of machinery, co-operative credit and so on.

The aid given by the State to small-scale industries in Indonesia is technical as well as financial, showing the importance of non-financial aid in any programme of assistance to them.

For small enterprises, the Banco Popular (People's Bank) was set up in Colombia in 1950, with private and State capital. One novel feature of the institution is that it not only gives loans to business-men for investment in production, but also to individuals, for consumption.

The financial systems in foreign countries, which have been evolved to assist small-scale industries offer useful lessons to India.

The foregoing study reveals a similarity between different countries in regard to the problems of small-scale industries, financial and non-financial.

In most countries examined above special institutions have had to be set up for the purpose. The state has also played a prominent part in directly and indirectly assisting small-scale industries. The study has pointed to the importance of external aids, apart from capital and credit, which are a pre-requisite for effective and fruitful financial assistance. Some outstanding features of note which have come to light are the credit guarantee and insurance, development of co-operatives, both for production and service, credit intelligence service, State patronage of small business and promotion of bank credit to small business through credit security and participation by other agencies.

Consistent with India's economic development and existing conditions, the lessons learnt from other countries could be applied to solve the problems of small-scale industries.

APPENDICES

Year	Value of Contracts Secured by Small Units with the Assistance of the Corporation (Rs.)
1955-56	4,67,750
1956-57	1,19,353
1957-58	62,14,964
1958-59	2,56,12,331
1959-60 (April-May)	19,78,666

Source: P. C. Basu, Managing Director, National Small Industries Corporation, "Role of Government in Assisting Small Industries—Assistance Rendered by the National Small Industries Corporation," *Agenda Papers, Item* IV (*d*), p. 3. Seminar on Financing of Small-Scale Industries in India, July 1959, Hyderabad, Reserve Bank of India.

Date	Total Number of Small-Scale Units Enlisted
31st March 1958[1]	1740
30th Sept. 1958[2]	2960
31st March 1959[3]	3935
July 1959[4]	4245

[1] *Agenda and Notes*, Eleventh Meeting of the Small Scale Industries Board, Ministry of Commerce and Industry, Government of India, May 1958, p. 104.

[2] *Agenda and Notes*, Twelfth Meeting of the Small Scale Industries Board, Ministry of Commerce and Industry, Government of India, November 1958, p. 108.

[3] *Agenda and Notes*, Thirteenth Meeting of the Small Scale Industries Board, Ministry of Commerce and Industry, Government of India, May 1959, p. 38.

[4] P. C. Basu, Managing Director, National Small Industries Corporation, "Role of Government in Assisting Small Industries—Assistance Rendered by the National Small Industries Corporation," *Agenda Papers, Item* IV (*d*), p. 2, Seminar on Financing of Smal-Scale Industries in India, July 1959, Hyderabad, Reserve Bank of India.

APPENDIX C

Particulars of applications received, orders placed and machines delivered are given below:

PROGRESSIVE TOTALS FROM INCEPTION OF THE SCHEME IN MARCH 1956

		As on 31-3-1957	As on 31-3-1958	As on 28-2-1959
I.	*Applications Received*			
	(i) No. of applications	984	1748	2083
	(ii) No. of machines	4090	7135	8263
	(iii) Value (Rs. lakhs)	262.12	501.77	608.40
II.	*Applications Accepted* (After rejections and withdrawals)			
	(i) No. of applications	661	1193	1476
	(ii) No. of machines	2459	4175	5259
	(iii) Value (Rs. lakhs)	165.44	339.39	447.23
III.	*Orders Placed*			
	(i) No. of machines	672	1898	3470
	(ii) Value (Rs. lakhs)	60.18	185.85	314.85
IV.	*Machines Delivered*			
	(i) No. of machines	191	978	2133
	(ii) Value (Rs. lakhs)	10.90	75.68	176.77

Source: Note on the Hire Purchase System, *Fourth Annual Report*, 1958-59, The National Small Industries Corporation, p. 3.

APPENDIX D

INCREASE IN OUTPUT AND EMPLOYMENT OF SMALL-SCALE UNITS AFTER INSTALLATION OF MACHINERY ON HIRE PURCHASE

Region	As on 31 March 1958			As on 30 Sept. 1958		
	No. of Units	Increase in Output per Month	Increase in Employment	No. of Units	Increase in Output per Month	Increase in Employment
1. Northern	49	2,20,896	525	75	3,27,196	670
2. Southern	22	93,593	76	118	N.R.	171
3. Western	28	1,01,043	119	101	1,22,843	217
4. Eastern	14	28,967	50	52	2,82,307	353
Total	113	4,44,499	770	346	7,32,346	1411

Source: Note on the Hire Purchase System, *Fourth Annual Report*, 1958-59. The National Small Industries Corporation.

APPENDIX E

1955-56	3601
1956-57	8108
1957-58	17978
1958-59	18710

Source: *Industrial Extension Service*, Small Scale Industries, April 1959, p. 4, Development Commissioner (Small Scale Industries), Ministry of Commerce and Industry, Government of India, New Delhi.

APPENDIX F

STATEMENT SHOWING INDUSTRY-WISE LOANS SANCTIONED BY THE STATE FINANCIAL CORPORATIONS TO SMALL-SCALE INDUSTRIAL UNITS AS ON 31 DECEMBER 1957*

(Rs. in lakhs)

Industry	*Amount*
1. Electricity supply and manufacture of electrical goods	10.91
2. General engineering and metal works	31.16
3. Pharmaceuticals and chemicals	8.97
4. Cold storage, food preservation and canning	45.94
5. Oil, rice and flour mills	18.80
6. Cotton ginning and pressing	5.85
7. Paper, paper board, stationery and printing	3.85
8. Manufacture of steel and steel goods	2.80
9. Cycle parts manufacture	3.15
10. Textiles and hosiery	13.25
11. Leather goods	0.60
12. Confectionery	3.05
13. Tea industry	13.35
14. Rubber, cashew-nut and coir	11.85
15. Miscellaneous	50.51
Total	224.04

* Excluding Andhra Pradesh State Financial Corporation and the Orissa State Financial Corporation.

Source: *Report of the Working Group on Industrial Co-operatives*, July 1958, Government of India, Ministry of Commerce and Industry, Table 5, p. 50.

APPENDIX G

LOANS SANCTIONED AND ADVANCED BY THE STATE FINANCIAL CORPORATIONS TO 372 SMALL-SCALE UNITS AS ON 31 DECEMBER 1958

	Name of the Corporation	No. of Applications Sanctioned	Amounts Sanctioned (Rs. '000)	Amounts Advanced (Rs. '000)
1.	Punjab Financial Corporation	73	50,28	29,27
2.	Kerala Financial Corporation	61	47,34	42,07
3.	Bombay Financial Corporation	67	53,12	27,35
4.	Andhra Pradesh Financial Corporation	60	27,70	19,44
5.	Assam Financial Corporation	19	14,25	8,16
6.	West Bengal Financial Corporation	5	9,35	3,90
7.	Uttar Pradesh Financial Corporation	29	19,82	17,47
8.	Bihar Financial Corporation	23	28,70	21,26
9.	Rajasthan Financial Corporation	13	7,15	2,68
10.	Madhya Pradesh Financial Corporation	11	10,40	1,50
11.	Orissa Financial Corporation	3	3,05	..
12.	Madras Industrial Investment Corp. Ltd. (as on 26-12-58)	8	8,25	8,17
	Total	372	2,79,41	1,81,27

Source: *Agenda and Notes*, Thirteenth Meeting of the Small Scale Industries Board, Hyderabad, May 1959, p. 60.

APPENDIX H

	Name of the State Financial Corporation	Difference between Amount Sanctioned and Advanced (Rs.)
1.	Bombay Financial Corporation	25,77,000
2.	Punjab Financial Corporation	21,01,000
3.	Madhya Pradesh Financial Corporation	8,90,000
4.	Andhra Pradesh Financial Corporation	8,26,000
5.	Bihar Financial Corporation	7,44,000
6.	Assam Financial Corporation	6,09,000
7.	West Bengal Financial Corporation	5,45,000
8.	Kerala Financial Corporation	5,27,000
9.	Rajasthan Financial Corporation	4,47,000
10.	Orissa Financial Corporation	3,05,000
11.	Uttar Pradesh Financial Corporation	2,35,000
12.	Madras Industrial Investment Corp. Ltd.	8,000

Source: *Agenda and Notes*, Thirteenth Meeting of the Small Scale Industries Board, Hyderabad, May 1959, p. 60.

BIBLIOGRAPHY

Report on Small Industries in India, International Planning Team, The Ford Foundation, Ministry of Finance, Government of India, 1955.

The Indian Industrial Commission Report, 1916-18.

P. C. Jain, *Problems in Indian Economics*, 1956.

The Journal of the Indian Institute of Bankers, April 1956.

The Journal of the Indian Institute of Bankers, October 1957.

G. M. Laud, *Co-operative Banking in India*, 1956.

Chitra and Viswanath, *Cottage Industries of India*, 1948.

L. C. Jain, *Indigenous Banking in India*, 1929.

All India Rural Credit Survey Report, Vol. III, 1954.

Advances to Small-Scale Industries: Pilot Scheme, State Bank of India, Central Office, Bombay, 1958.

Small-Scale Industries: Pilot Scheme, State Bank of India; *Information for Borrowers*, State Bank of India, Central Office, Bombay, 1958.

J. C. De, Deputy Secretary and Treasurer, Ministry of Commerce and Consumers Industries, Government of India, "A Note on the Pilot Scheme for the Provision of Credit to Small-Scale Industries in Madras Circle," 18 April 1959.

Pilot Scheme for Assistance to Small-Scale Industries, State Bank of India.

Case Studies in Small Industries Finance, State Bank of India, May 1959.

"Pilot Scheme of the State Bank of India for Provision of Credit to Small-Scale Industries," *Background Papers* 4, Seminar on Financing of Small-Scale Industries in India, July 1959, Hyderabad, Reserve Bank of India.

Report of the Working Group on Industrial Cooperatives, Ministry of Commerce and Industry, Government of India, July 1958.

F. A. Ryan, Assistant Director, Small Industries Service Institute, Bombay, *Industrial Credit by the State Bank—An Appraisal*.

"A Note Prepared in the Reserve Bank on The Financial System of Japan with Special Reference to Financing of Small-Scale Industries," *Background Papers* 13, Seminar on Financing of

69

Small-Scale Industries in India, July 1959, Hyderabad, Reserve Bank of India.

"A Note Prepared in the Reserve Bank on Special Institutions for the Finance of Small Business in Foreign Countries," *Background Papers* 12, Seminar on Financing of Small-Scale Industries in India, July 1959, Hyderabad, Reserve Bank of India.

Federal Policies and Programmes that Benefit Small Business, Prepared for the Cabinet Committee on Small Business, Department of Commerce and Small Business Administration, 23 September 1957.

Institutions for Industrial Finance and Development, Lok Sabha Secretariat, *A Brief Survey of the Special Organizational Set-ups in Some Selected Countries*, 1955.

Rao, K. Vasudeva, Deputy Chief Officer, Industrial Finance Department, Reserve Bank of India, "Institutional Set-up. Long-term Credit Institutions such as State Financial Corporations," *Agenda Papers, Item* II (*d*), Seminar on Financing of Small-Scale Industries in India, July 1959, Hyderabad, Reserve Bank of India.

The Sixth Annual Report, 31 March 1959, The Kerala Financial Corporation.

Menon, P. K. Krishnan Kutti, Chairman, Board of Directors, Kerala Financial Corporation, "Speech," Sixth Annual General Meeting, 26 June 1959.

The Mysore State Financial Corporation: How It Functions.

Report of the Board of Directors for the Period Ended 31 March 1959, The West Bengal Financial Corporation, Calcutta, 1959.

Fourth Annual Report and Accounts for the Year Ended 31 March 1959, Uttar Pradesh Financial Corporation.

Fourth Annual Report, 31 March 1959, Bihar State Financial Corporation.

Sinha, Rajendra, Chairman, "Speech," Fourth Annual General Meeting, 29 June 1959, Bihar State Financial Corporation.

Fifth Annual Report and Accounts for the Year Ended 31 March 1959, Assam Financial Corporation.

Assam Financial Corporation: What It Is and How It Functions, March 1955.

First Annual Report and Accounts, 31 March 1958, Orissa State Financial Corporation.

Second Annual Report and Accounts, 31 March 1959, Orissa State Financial Corporation.

Orissa State Financial Corporation: What It Means to You, 1959.

Fourth Annual Report, 31 March 1959, Rajasthan Financial Corporation.

Podar, Ramnath A., Chairman, "Speech," Fourth Annual General Meeting, 29 June 1959, The Rajasthan Financial Corporation.

Rajasthan Financial Corporation: How it Helps? and How It Works? 1955.

Second Annual Report, 31 March 1958, Bombay State Financial Corporation.

Third Annual Report, 31 March 1959, Bombay State Financial Corporation.

Finance For Your Small-Scale Industry, Bombay State Financial Corporation, 1957.

Bombay State Financial Corporation: What It Means To You, 1958.

Second Annual Report, 1955-56, Hyderabad State Financial Corporation.

Hyderabad State Financial Corporation: How It Helps Industrial Development.

First Annual Report, 1956-57, Andhra Pradesh State Financial Corporation.

Second Annual Report, 1957-58, Andhra Pradesh State Financial Corporation.

Third Annual Report, 1958-59, Andhra Pradesh State Financial Corporation.

Andhra Pradesh State Financial Corporation: How It Helps Industrial Development in the State, 1959.

Third Annual Report and Accounts, 31 March 1958, Madhya Pradesh Financial Corporation.

Fourth Annual Report and Accounts, 31 March 1959, Madhya Pradesh Financial Corporation.

Chairman's Speech: Third Annual General Meeting, 24 June 1958, Madhya Pradesh Financial Corporation.

Chairman's Speech: Fourth Annual General Meeting, 27 June 1959, Madhya Pradesh Financial Corporation.

Madhya Pradesh Financial Corporation, "Brochure."

First Annual Report and Accounts, 31 March 1954, Punjab Financial Corporation.

Second Annual Report and Accounts, 31 March 1955, Punjab Financial Corporation.

Third Annual Report and Accounts, 31 March 1956, Punjab Financial Corporation.

Fourth Annual Report and Accounts, 31 March 1957, Punjab Financial Corporation.

Fifth Annual Report and Accounts, 31 March 1958, Punjab Financial Corporation.

Sixth Annual Report and Accounts, 31 March 1959, Punjab Financial Corporation.

You and P.F.C., Punjab Financial Corporation.

"State Financial Corporations in India," *Background Papers*, Seminar on Financing of Small-Scale Industries in India, July 1959, Hyderabad, Reserve Bank of India.

Agenda and Notes, Eleventh Meeting of the Small Scale Industries Board, Ministry of Commerce and Industry, Government of India, May 1958.

Agenda and Notes, Twelfth Meeting of the Small Scale Industries Board, Vol. I, Ministry of Commerce and Industry, Government of India, November 1958.

Agenda and Notes, Thirteenth Meeting of the Small Scale Industries Board, Ministry of Commerce and Industry, Government of India, May 1959.

Minutes, Eleventh Meeting of the Small Scale Industries Board, Ministry of Commerce and Industry, Government of India, May 1958.

Minutes, Twelfth Meeting of the Small Scale Industries Board, Ministry of Commerce and Industry, Government of India, November 1958.

Minutes, Thirteenth Meeting of the Small Scale Industries Board, Ministry of Commerce and Industry, Government of India, May 1959.

Bulletin of Small Industries, October 1958, Published by the Development Commissioner (Small Scale Industries), Ministry of Commerce and Industries, Government of India.

Bulletin of Small Industries No. 9, November 1958, Published by the Development Commissioner (Small Scale Industries), Ministry of Commerce and Industries, Government of India.

Bulletin of Small Industries No. 14, April 1959, Published by the

Development Commissioner (Small Scale Industries), Ministry of Commerce and Industries, Government of India.

Bulletin of Small Industries No. 18, August 1959, Published by the Development Commissioner (Small Scale Industries), Ministry of Commerce and Industries, Government of India.

Bulletin of Small Industries No. 6, August 1958, Published by the Development Commissioner (Small Scale Industries), Ministry of Commerce and Industries, Government of India.

Bulletin of Small Industries No. 15, May 1959, Published by the Development Commissioner (Small Scale Industries), Ministry of Commerce and Industries, Government of India.

Bulletin of Small Industries No. 3, May 1958, Published by the Development Commissioner (Small Scale Industries), Ministry of Commerce and Industries, Government of India.

"A Note prepared by the Reserve Bank on the Procedure Being Followed by the Various State Directorate of Industries for Disbursing Loans to Small-Scale Industries under the State Aid to Industries Acts/Rules etc.," *Background Papers* 8, Seminar on Financing of Small-Scale Industries in India, July 1959, Hyderabad, Reserve Bank of India.

"Small-Scale Industries Board," *Background Papers* 9, Seminar on Financing of Small-Scale Industries in India, July 1959, Hyderabad, Reserve Bank of India.

"The National Small Industries Corporation," *Background Papers* 10, Seminar on Financing of Small-Scale Industries in India, July 1959, Hyderabad, Reserve Bank of India.

Small Industries Corporations: *A Brief Survey* (4 February 1955 to 31 August 1956), the National Small Industries Corporation, New Delhi.

Basu, P. C., Managing Director, National Small Industries Corporation, "Role of Government in Assisting Small Industries— Assistance Rendered by the National Small Industries Corporation," *Agenda Papers* IV (*d*), Seminar on Financing of Small-Scale Industries in India, July 1959, Hyderabad, Reserve Bank of India.

Third Annual Report, 1957-58, The National Small Industries Corporation.

Machinery on Hire-Purchase: *General Terms and Conditions*, The National Small Industries Corporation.

"Note on the Hire-Purchase System," *Fourth Annual Report*, 1958-59, The National Small Industries Corporation.

"Industrial Estates," *Background Papers* II, Seminar on Financing of Small-Scale Industries in India, July 1959, Hyderabad, Reserve Bank of India.

Small Industries Information Series No. 2, Industrial Estates Development Commissioner (Small Scale Industries), Ministry of Commerce and Consumers Industries, Government of India.

Who's Who, Industrial Estate, Guindy, Madras, May 1959.

Industrial Estate, Guindy, Issued by the Director of Industries and Commerce, Government of Madras.

Industrial Extension Service, April 1959, Published by Development Commissioner (Small Scale Industries), Ministry of Commerce and Industry, Government of India.

"Role of Government in Providing Financial and Technical Assistance to Small-Scale industries," *Background Papers* 7, Seminar on Financing of Small-Scale Industries in India, July 1959, Hyderabad, Reserve Bank of India.

Rao, T. S., Deputy Chief Officer, Agricultural Credit Department, Reserve Bank of India, "Institutional Set-up: Co-operative Banks," *Agenda Papers Item* II (*c*), Seminar on Financing of Small-Scale Industries in India, July, 1959, Hyderabad, Reserve Bank of India.

"A Note Prepared by the Reserve Bank of India on Commercial Bank Finance to Medium and Small-Scale Business Units," *Background Papers* 6, Seminar on Financing of Small-Scale Industries in India, July 1959, Hyderabad, Reserve Bank of India.

Shah, C. K., "Commercial Banks and Finance for Small Industries in India," *The Journal of the Indian Institute of Bankers*, October 1957.

Dhar, P. N., *Small Scale Industries in Delhi—A Study in Investment, Output and Employment Aspects*, Delhi School of Economics, University of Delhi, 1958.

Chandavarkar, S. V., Staff Officer, State Bank of India, "Institutional Set-up: Commercial Banks," *Agenda Papers* II (*b*), Seminar on Financing of Small-Scale Industries in India, July 1959, Hyderabad, Reserve Bank of India.

Capital for Medium and Small Scale Industries, Society for Social and Economic Studies, 1959.

The Hindu, 5 November 1959.

INDEX

75